World of
DOGS

World of
DOGS

Wendy Boorer

Ω OMEGA BOOKS

Contents

Series edited by Howard Loxton
Picture research by Ann Davies

This edition published 1983 by Omega Books Ltd,
1 West Street, Ware, Hertfordshire, under licence
from the proprietor.

Copyright © 1976 Elsevier Publishing Projects SA, Lausanne.

ISBN 0 907853 29 3

Printed and bound in Hong Kong by South China Printing Co.

Introduction

Man's relationship with the dog is unlike that he has with any other animal.
It offers him his loyalty and his energy and in return has earned man's love.
In the thousands of years since the partnership began the prehistoric, wolf-like
animal has been developed by man into an enormous variety of specialized breeds
and learned to serve man in all manner of ways.

This book presents some of the many roles in which the dog may now be found
around the world and shows the reader some aspects of its many faceted character.
But most of all it seeks to share with you the delight which dogs can bring into
man's life and the pleasure that can come from learning more about them.

In Search of the Dog

We do not know how it all began, that long association between man and the dog, the most widely used and the oldest domesticated animal. The evidence seems to suggest that twenty thousand years or so ago man was a nomadic hunter living in small bands and preying on the migratory herds of grazing animals. The success of these small tribes of hunters depended on their awareness of animal behavior. The wolf-like creature who was to become the domesticated dog lived much the same sort of life—also intensely aware of the other animals around him.

Since they have come to share their lives modern man has apparently become intelligent at the expense of this sense of awareness, but the modern dog often seems to be intelligent because he is still in tune with nature in this way.

"He understands every word I say," is a claim often made by fond owners who have been amazed at their dog's quick grasp of a situation. But a dog's ability to understand what is going on is not based on linguistic ability. Words as such mean nothing. They are sounds without association until the dog has been taught them by repetition in a certain situation. By persistent repetition it is possible to get a dog to understand perhaps forty commands, a very far cry from "understanding every word." However, although dog owners may tend

to think that the only way they communicate with their animals is through words, their dogs know otherwise.

The main reason that many dogs are able to anticipate their owner's next move is because they have seen the small involuntary signs that invariably precede a particular event. The person who makes them is often unaware of these signals, but they are very clear to the dog whose eyesight is particularly acute in picking out and interpreting small significant movements.

On the whole the dog's sight is poor compared with our own. The dog cannot see color, and unmoving objects at any distance remain unnoticed, but the slightest flicker of movement immediately focuses the animal's attention. This is the legacy of the past when the dog was a hunter and such movement signified food. Although the dog does not understand sentences or conversations it is very sensitive to tones of voice and this is another way in which an owner involuntarily communicates with his pet. A dog's hearing has a much wider range and is a great deal more acute than that of man. In particular the dog can distinguish between much smaller intervals of sound than we can. It is this particular refinement that enables a dog to pick out familiar footsteps long before any other member of the household hears them, or to recognize

Right: Dogs are social animals used to the discipline of pack living. This is the reason for their success as pets. Here a young Newfoundland keeps an eye on the crowds around him.

Left: Amongst a host of terrier breeds, most of whom are cheerful extroverts, the Sealyham Terrier is one who is claimed by his admirers to have an extra special sense of humour.

the noise of a particular automobile engine even in the midst of other traffic. The dog's hearing covers a much wider range than ours. It is possible to buy "silent" dog whistles, the frequency of which is too high for the human ear but dogs can hear them perfectly well.

Because the dog's hearing is so sensitive all good dog trainers have something of the actor's ability to use tone to convey emotion. The dog will jump to the forceful word of command whereas the same word drawled in a lackadaisical way will achieve nothing. Praise too must be enthusiastic for it is the tone, not the words, which tell a dog whether he has done right or wrong.

Watching a dog when it is out will soon show what an important part smell plays in its life, for the dog spends a great deal of time sniffing and evaluating the information gained by its nose. The dog's sense of smell is so infinitely superior to our own that it is extremely difficult for us to appreciate just how much the dog learns from scent. The olfactory membrane, the olfactory nerve and the part of the brain dealing with smell are all highly developed. Smells that instinctively interest a dog are urine, the secretions of the anal glands, the oestrus odor of a bitch in season, food and the trail left by a possible prey. However this list can certainly be modified and added to by training. One of the more sophisticated skills which man has taught the dog is to find things which man cannot locate, from mines in a minefield to hidden heroin or people buried in an avalanche. Many dogs of hound type are trained to pick out and follow a particular scent at the expense of all others. Foxhounds chase foxes and coonhounds chase racoons and it would

Left: The more young puppies see of the world, the more confident they are likely to become. This Yorkshire Terrier puppy has yet to grow its adult coat.

Right: A little mongrel with a passion for hunting. Hunting in long grass calls for a specialized technique consisting of a series of long bounds when the dog pounces with stiffly outstretched forepaws hoping to pin down a scampering titbit.

Below left: A gate like this presents no obstacle to an active dog.

Below: When two strange dogs meet they go through certain canine rituals. The stance of these two and the angle of their tails suggest that they are confident well-adjusted individuals who will end up playing boisterous games rather than fighting.

The sledge dogs of the north probably live the hardest lives of all working animals. They spend day and night without shelter of any kind and, as well as working under harsh conditions, have often been subjected to brutal treatment. They are fed on frozen seal meat, a food rich in fats which undoubtedly helps to maintain the very thick coat necessary for their survival. The generic name for all these dogs is husky, believed to be a corruption of "esky," a slang diminutive of Eskimo. There are, however, several recognized breeds, the best known being the Alaskan Malamute and the Siberian Husky. Rather naturally, considering their working conditions, huskies have a reputation for ferocity but, if treated with consideration, they are no more unreliable than any other breed of dog. They are powerful, strongwilled animals who need firm handling and a great deal of exercise.

In the past the Huskies' role has been strictly utilitarian but they are now exhibited and used for the increasingly popular sport of sledge dog racing in North America. For these races a single file of dogs is hitched to a lightweight sledge. The more usual method of harnessing is in pairs with a leader in front. It has been suggested that the day of the dog sledge is over and that motorized transport will replace it. Although this seemed to be inevitable, the oil crisis and economic conditions in general suggest that predictions of the huskies' complete disuse may have been premature.

be inconceivable that either should be interested in the prey of the other. Scientific investigation has proved the dog's ability to distinguish scent in minute quantities, but any owner of a bitch in season who has had every stray dog for miles around homing in on her, will not need convincing on this point. Bloodhounds are the most remarkable of the scenting hounds, but even they get confused by the trails of identical twins, although they can relate the trail to the twin who laid it when they catch up with them both. An animal who gains so much information through its nose is also bound to leave a large number of scent signals to be interpreted by others of its species. The male dog urinates on almost every upright object that it passes. This is not with the intention of emptying its bladder (something a dog hardly ever does) but in order to leave signals for any other dog that goes that way. It is very difficult to guess all the significance of these scent signals to another dog. A bitch in season will squat every few yards in order to leave a trail by which male dogs can find her. A dog will mark out its own territory with monotonous regularity. Indeed owners are sometimes horrified when moving house to find that their normally house-trained

Above: Dogs dig to bury surplus food, or to enlarge burrows, or—like anyone else on the beach—just for fun!
Right: All dogs enjoy bones which should be large and uncooked if they are not to cause digestive trouble.
Below: One of the world's most successful dogs in a number of roles is the Labrador Retriever. Their kindly, reliable temperament makes them excellent pets. This is a yellow but black, and more rarely, liver are also acceptable colors.

animal has cocked his leg in every unfamiliar room. They do not recognize this instinctive behavior by which a dog asserts its right to territorial space. A dog will defecate and then scratch earth very vigorously over the spot to make the mark even more noticeable to other passing canines. All these rituals are part of the social life of all dogs.

By observing dogs' behavior at a distance a great deal can be deduced about individual temperament. Two strange dogs meeting in a friendly fashion will first pause at a distance with tails waving gaily in the air. They will then trot confidently towards each other to meet briefly face to face before circling to sniff each other's rear. They will then cock their legs over the nearest upright surface before continuing on their way. A nervous dog will crouch when approached by another. With its tail tightly clamped between its legs it will not let any stranger sniff its rear, continually circling so that

its head is always towards the unknown. An aggressive dog will approach with head and tail held still and upright and with a peculiar stiff, stilted walk. A fight may develop quite suddenly and be over equally quickly if one dog runs away or submits by rolling over and exposing voluntarily the vulnerable throat. Fighting methods differ with different breeds. Some dogs have the instinct to bite and hang on chewing their way steadily through whatever they have sunk their teeth into. Others try to slam into their opponent thus bowling them over and exposing the vulnerable throat and stomach. Yet others dash in and out trying to slash and cripple their adversary.

Many facets of dog behavior are only partially understood. What we do know is that in the wild state the dog lives under the rule imposed by survival in the pack and, in modern society, the dog is happiest as a disciplined member of a family unit.

Above: This Long-haired Dachshund puppy has rolled over on its back in a gesture of complete submission to the older Dachshund. Such behavior is typical of what happens when a young puppy meets a strange adult. The exposure of the younger dog's vulnerable throat and unprotected abdomen inhibits the adult from any act of agression.

Left: A yellow Labrador Retriever puppy ventures across the top of a canal lock gate.

Above: Much sheepdog behavior is instinctive: even as pets many of them still want to round things up and may spend their walks continually circling the people with them in an attempt to keep them together. This looks like a group of dogs making the most of their morning exercise to play a racing, chasing game but, in fact, the Bearded Collie on the right is making a vain attempt to keep all the other dogs together in a neat and tidy flock.

Right: Fights can start for any number of reasons and a serious fight is practically impossible to stop single handed. Sometimes dogs playing can accidentally hurt each other and this can trigger off an explosion. The worst fights are usually those caused by jealousy—over a treasured possession, an owner's affection, or a bitch in season.

Dogs who are habitual fighters can be divided into three classes. There are those who are nervous and attack in fear. These are often created by owners who are fearful that other dogs may be agressive. There are over possessive dogs who will attack other dogs that enter their territory or come near their owners. This is an over developed guarding instinct that can be a great nuisance. The third category fight because they enjoy it. Although the first two kinds of fighters can be improved by the right training the third sort are incorrigible.

It's a Show Dog's Life

How does the life of a show dog compare with that of a family pet? Some show dogs of course *are* pets, and when at home snooze by the fire and go for enthusiastic walks, like any other family dog, but the majority are kennel dogs for the very simple reason that most exhibitors have too many animals for them to be kept any other way. Serious dog breeders often will keep as a house pet a breed with which they are unconnected in the show ring. This is a sort of safety valve, enabling them to maintain a critical distance between themselves and their show team, who need to be viewed dispassionately rather than with sentiment.

The kennel dog tends to live a very well ordered existence, being let out and exercised and fed, all at set times, as the kennel staff work through the day's schedule. The dogs are often kenneled in pairs as solitary dogs are often noisy as well as bored. Groups of dogs are not usually kept together because they sometimes gang up on the weakest member, and some of the fighting breeds have to live alone as there is always a risk when two or more are together. Dogs do better where they can see and hear a lot of what is going on,

for boredom can create problems. Some dogs become very destructive while others develop habits like coat chewing which is never seen in dogs kept unconfined. All dogs are individuals so pairing kennel companions needs a certain amount of care.

Picking a puppy for show is very much a lottery even for an experienced breeder. Having bred a litter with show potential, the ideal would be to run all the puppies on until they are old enough for a critical judgement to be made with more certainty than can be done at eight weeks. However this is rarely financially possible so a choice must be made at an age when many faults have not

Left: The egg-shaped head and the lamb-like appearance of the Bedlington Terrier are achieved by careful shaping of the coat with scissors. Although angelic to look at, with a soft, dark, gentle eye, these dogs are as hard bitten and game as any other terrier.
Below: Dogs going to shows often travel very long distances, like these three Airedales, who have journeyed comfortably in the back of a station wagon. They learn early in life to mix peaceably with their fellows.

had time to show. Most people will try to keep two puppies who can grow up together, playing with and amusing each other. These dogs will be reared with great care because they will be judged upon their conformation, and this depends on their early environment as well as their inherited characteristics. Their diet may be monotonous compared with the pet dog but it will be scientifically balanced and contain vitamin and mineral supplements in the right amounts for maximum skeletal growth as many breed standards call for good heavy bone in the adult animal.

Young hopefuls destined for the show ring will be kept in clean airy surroundings with plenty of space for play, but their show training will start almost immediately. The ideal show dog will stand in the ring, poised, alert, radiating confidence and expectancy, a pose which draws every eye towards him. Some dogs are natural showmen but most have to be taught the art slowly and patiently. Without self confidence there can be no showmanship, so everything is done to ensure that the young dog develops a sound reliable temperament.

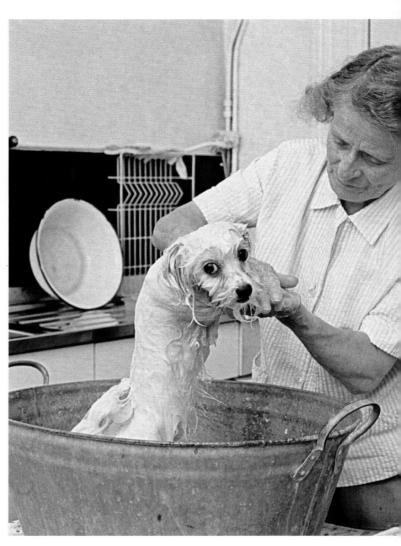

Puppies brought up amid noise and bustle very rarely exhibit nervousness. If their background is normally quiet they must be taken out and about and introduced to as many new sights and sounds as possible. Being kept among numbers of dogs, they will be used to meeting them in quantity and will be encouraged to be neither over effusive nor over aggressive. Every effort will be made to give them individual human attention and in particular they will be taught to stand in a show pose from the very earliest age. For a short period each day the dog is placed and held in the position that shows it to the best advantage. With small breeds that are customarily judged on the table, this lesson will take place on a bench or box. Gradually the dog is encouraged to adopt the stance on its own and hold it for longer periods. It is then taught to accept

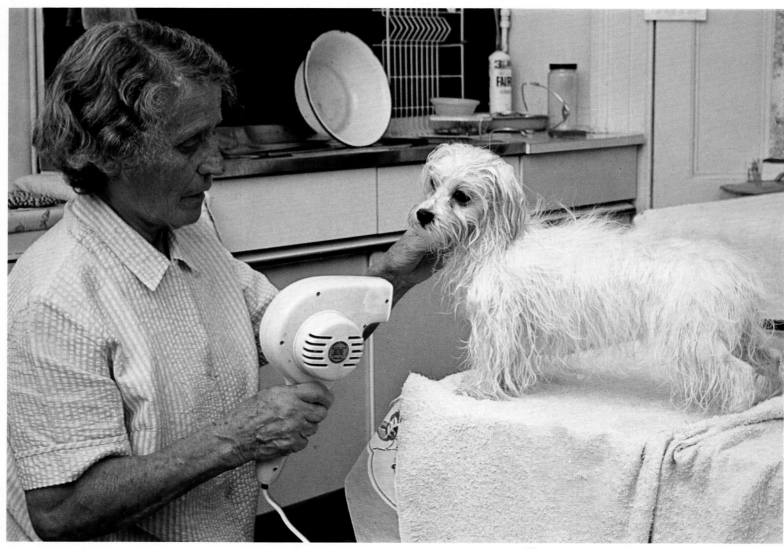

Opposite page: Bathing is a part of every show dog's routine. With all white breeds, like the Maltese, a bath is essential before every show. A hair dryer is the quickest and most efficient way of drying a toy dog's coat. Many dogs find the process a little alarming at first but gentle reassurance will produce the sort of confidence shown here.

Left and above: The coat of a Yorkshire Terrier requires constant attention to preserve its length. The coat is oiled to promote its growth and then rolled up in paper of soft fabric "crackers" which are secured with an elastic band. The coat and moustaches of a show Yorkshire Terrier should be long enough to trail along the ground. To achieve such perfection of coat needs constant skilled care.

Above: The trimming of a terrier for the show ring is a skill only gained by practice and experience. The dogs are accustomed to being groomed on a table and this Scottish Terrier is attached by its collar to a grooming stand while final adjustments are made to its outline before it enters the ring. Grooming tables, equipment and stands are all part of the exhibitor's luggage.

Above right: The owners of Old English Sheepdogs also put in a great deal of hard work before their dogs enter the ring. The sheets spread out on the ground are to prevent the dogs getting stained by grass or mud.

Right: A Shetland Sheepdog receives its final brushing. The concentration on the owner's face is an indication of the seriousness with which showing is taken.

Far right: These Salukis are tied up on English style benching. All the larger shows are benched so that the dogs, when they are not being judged, shall be on display to the public. Most dogs soon become used to the idea and spend much of their time on the bench fast asleep.

inspection by a stranger who will run his hands over the animal, assessing conformation and condition. They will also learn to have their mouth opened and their teeth inspected. Regular tooth care will be part of their lives for it is important not only that a show dog's teeth are positioned correctly, they must also be healthy, clean and white.

Parallel with the training to stand for examination in the show ring, the young dog will also receive training in how to show its movement to the best advantage. Correct movement is not the same for all breeds but it is always demonstrated in the same way. The dog is required to trot beside its owner, moving smartly in a straight line on a loose lead. This too requires time and patience to teach, for the animal must neither pull nor hang back, and even progressing

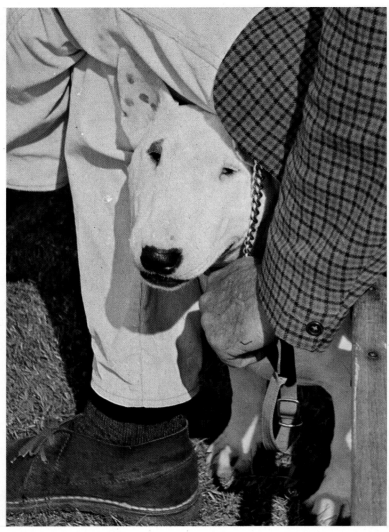

in a straight line is more difficult than it appears to the onlooker. Clever owners will judge to a nicety the speed of the dog and adjust their own accordingly, for some paces will suit some individuals more than others.

The sparkle of perfect health and condition is achieved by good feeding and plenty of exercise. Ears and teeth are inspected regularly and cleaned if necessary. Toenails are clipped short if they need it, for long nails encourage the feet to spread, and for many show dogs attention to their coats will be a daily task. The time needed for grooming and trimming varies tremendously from breed to breed. Some breeds require very specialized and lengthy coat care. The fine, silky coat of the Yorkshire Terrier is a case in point. In the adult dog this coat is so long that it sweeps the ground, and this terrier breed is traditionally shown standing on its travelling box so that the length of coat can be seen to advantage. To prevent the ends of the hair becoming split or broken off, the hair is divided into locks and each lock rolled up in tissue paper and secured with a rubber band. Just before showing the hair is brushed out to fall in a shining cascade.

The coat of the Puli has to be twisted and encouraged to hang in a mass of cords. Afghans, Old English Sheepdogs and Pekinese need hours of dedicated brushing to show them off to perfection. The Kerry Blue Terrier and the Bedlington Terrier have their outline sculpted by scissors. A craftsman in trimming can minimize many faults in dog's construction by leaving a little extra hair on in one place and taking it off in another. Poodles are clipped into the required Lion clip but the mane and pom poms need regular and careful brushing to prevent matting. The majority

Much of a show dog's day consists of waiting and the dog must learn to wait patiently in all kinds of situations.
Far left: This Old English Sheepdog, waiting for its turn in the ring, does not have to have its coat trimmed but it needs plenty of grooming to prevent it matting. The white areas are heavily chalked to emphasise the color. His head has been combed to show the eye which is normally entirely covered.
Left: The English Bull Terrier is now a gentleman, having lived down a ruffianly past when it was bred solely for fighting. The dark triangular eye now views the world with a humorous twinkle rather than an aggressive glare.
Below, far left: Soft-coated Wheaten Terriers waiting by the ringside.
Below, centre: The Wire Fox Terrier, although no longer popular as a pet dog, is still a big winner at shows.
Below: The best of breed in Samoyeds relaxes with its owner.

of terriers need stripping and trimming to maintain the distinctive outline of each breed. This is best done by plucking out the old hair between finger and thumb, although stripping combs and scissors are also used.

Many of the long haired breeds will automatically be bathed before each show so it is not surprising that some will arrive wearing trousers and raincoats to protect the hours of work put in by their owners. Nor is it surprising that the state of a dog's coat is often the topic of exhibitor's conversation, and that shampoos, conditioners and remedies for coat troubles abound.

Show dogs have to be good travellers. A dog that is continually sick on the way to a show is unlikely to be looking and feeling its best when being judged. Young show prospects are introduced to automobiles early in life so that they have plenty of opportunity to become relaxed and confident travelers. Toy dogs and terriers, who very often travel in boxes or crates, are accustomed to them from puppyhood, being shut up in them for a short while each day so that they are used to the idea. All show dogs have to learn to stay quietly when tied up so that they can be left on the benches without making a fuss.

Experienced exhibitors taking a young dog to his first show will do everything that they can to make sure that the dog enjoys the trip. For many kennel dogs a show is a day out with more fuss and attention and human company than usual. To show a dog for a number of years keeping his interest and alertness alive in the ring requires ingenuity and perseverance from his handler but is all part of the mystique of showmanship.

Above: Judging can be a very strenuous day's work. Each dog has to be examined very carefully and some judges will have more than a hundred specimens paraded before them in a day.
Right: The watchful glance of a Staffordshire Bull Terrier suggests it is not a dog to be trifled with. The very prominent cheek muscles and the powerful jaws are those of a dog with a punishing bite—but the show dog must learn to show perfect manners before the judges.
Above right: A Smooth Fox Terrier stands on the table ready to be examined by the judge.
Far right: When a dog has won the event deserves to be recorded. Here a Rough Collie has its photograph taken. It may be needed to advertise the owner's kennel, for the dog's stud card, or just to hang on the wall, but there is enough demand for several specialist dog photographers to attend every big show. These people are skilled in taking pictures of show dogs which make the most of the dog's virtues and minimize its faults.

The Versatile German Shepherd

The German Shepherd dog is by far the most popular dog in the world. Everyone knows of the breed and opinions differ sharply as to its merits. German Shepherd owners are a devoted band of enthusiasts in whose eyes the breed is supreme, both in looks and intelligence. Others look on these dogs with suspicion, mindful of the many notorious newspaper reports billing the breed as a savage killer. The exploits of the German Shepherd have attracted so much attention from journalists that few people can remain indifferent to the dog.

How did this saint or sinner image come about? The truth is that what are outstanding merits in the trained animal with the right master can become dangerous liabilities in the untrained and bored dog with an irresponsible owner. It is also true that in any breed that becomes very popular, temperament is liable to suffer. The demand for puppies is so great that unsuitable animals are used as breeding stock and dogs unreliable and nervous in temperament, as well as poor in conformation, contribute to the breed's bad name.

Possibly more than any other dog, the German Shepherd resembles the wolf in looks and this has led to confusion in the mind of the public who believe that wolf blood is the reason for the breed's reputation for savagery. This idea has received further impetus from the unfortunate fact that the German Shepherd was misguidedly called the Alsatian Wolf Dog when it was introduced into Britain and a number of other countries. No modern breed of dog however has any connection with the modern wolf and such crosses, though theoretically possible, would be unthinkable to anyone seriously interested in a breed's welfare.

The breed is not a very old one and the credit for the outstanding merits of the animal, which make it the most versatile of working dogs, must go to the German fanciers of some seventy or eighty years ago who established the German Shepherd as we know it today. Sheepdogs from the areas of Wurttemburg and Thuringia provided the basis for the breed. Animals like these were used, not only to protect sheep, but also to prevent the flocks straying into arable land. In other words these dogs had to be virtually tireless and able to act on their own initiative. The present day success of the German Shepherd is due very much to these two requirements. The dog is a strong and agile one with an effortless springy gait, which enables

Left: The German Shepherd is often used as a guard and security dog. Troublemakers are less likely to pick a quarrel when there is a large and powerful dog to contend with, such as the dog which greets guests at this hotel.

Right: The breed's best known role is, nevertheless, that of companion and member of the family. A dog of sound temperament brought up with children often displays a very protective maternal role towards them. Showing the greatest patience with a baby's attempts at learning to walk, the dog will often put up with indignities it would not tolerate from an adult member of the family. In return, however, children should be taught to respect the animal's right to a certain amount of peace and quiet.

it to glide along, covering plenty of ground with each stride. The hairs of the coat are short but very dense and weather resistant. This means that the dog can work in any climate, as this type of coat acts as an insulator for both extremes of heat and cold. German breeders have always recognized that temperament is of equal importance to conformation in a working dog. The combination which makes the German Shepherd supreme is alertness, reliability and the power of concentration. Indeed, when trying to forecast the success of training any dog, it is this ability to concentrate, allied with the desire to please, which produces the best results. The breed was scarcely known outside its native land before the first World War. However, both the police and the German army appreciated their worth and they were used on the battlefield as messenger dogs, and as rescue dogs to find the wounded. This brought them to the attention of both British and United States soldiers who took specimens of the breed home to both countries. In the 1920s the German Shepherd enjoyed a phenomenal rise in popularity. Then, as more and more dogs got into inexperienced ownership, mismanaged and bored animals brought the breed into disrepute. They were labeled as savage and treacherous and there was an equally phenomenal slump in their numbers. Since then they have increased

An active and energetic breed, the German Shepherd needs plenty of exercise and jumping is one good way of getting it. Its strength and agility are very important in police and army work. Dogs employed by such forces are taught to scramble over a six foot scale jump but no dog that is not fully fit is capable of such a jump or should be asked to face such an obstacle. When teaching dogs to jump it is very important to make the early stages easy, pleasant and successful. Since the jump will get progressively higher, and the dog will be asked to make more and more effort, he must learn to enjoy jumping on command. To be successful he must receive plenty of praise in the early stages.

slowly and steadily until they are now the premier breed in the world both as working animals and as companions. Primarily when one thinks of the German Shepherd one thinks of a police dog. The more dramatic aspects of police work such as chasing and stopping the criminal, are probably the least important aspect of the dog's work. Their value as a deterrent is their greatest asset. Not only are they an added protection to the patrolman on his beat, the threat of sending in the dogs has caused many a suspect to surrender. Police dogs are used in crowd control and to search buildings where criminals may be hidden. Regular patrols of parks, building sites and public institutions help prevent thefts and vandalism. Air Forces use these dogs to patrol airfields and

A fully grown German Shepherd Dog is in many ways physically superior to man. Their hearing and scenting abilities are much greater. They can run faster and jump higher. Police dog training utilizes these advantages to help keep law and order. The skills which training develops can also be put to less serious use. As a change from patrolling airfields this Air Force police dog is put through its paces to entertain the public.

Teaching a dog to climb ladders, negotiate cat-walks or climb under obstacles, a standard part of police dog training, not only increases its own ability to work in all kinds of locations but also builds up confidence in its handler as a leader.

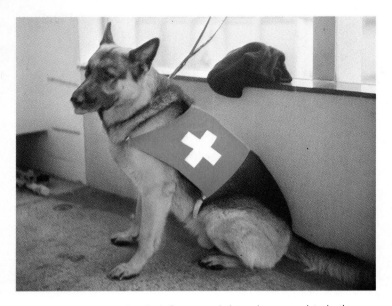

Above: Dogs trained for Red Cross work have been used in both World Wars to find wounded and to carry medical supplies.

Below: Police dogs are taught to attack on command and, perhaps more important, to stop when told to do so.

Right: As a guide dog for the blind the German Shepherd has proved immensely valuable. These dogs do not start their training until they are fully adult and are put through a series of rigorous tests to weed out those who will be temperamentally unsuitable. Amongst the qualities looked for are a willingness to please and an absence of nervousness. There are two aspects of the dog's work which often seem miraculous to observers and which are the result of months of careful training. One is the dog's ability to gauge the height and width of both itself and its blind owner when negotiating obstacles. The other is the dog's skill in taking its owner amongst traffic. To cross roads safely the guide dog must learn to ignore its master's command of "forward" until there is no moving vehicle within a dangerous distance. Instead of implicit obedience, which is all that is asked of most trained animals, the guide dog must learn to discriminate as to whether it is safe to obey a command or not.

munition dumps. Given the right conditions a dog can scent a hidden stranger a hundred yards away. Many frontier posts have dog patrols and dogs have been attached to American Army units to warn the soldiers of the approach of guerillas.

It would be difficult to substantiate a claim that the German Shepherd has better scenting ability than any other breed, but their willingness and determination make them good tracking dogs. They have searched for—and found—lost children. They work with customs officials detecting smuggled drugs. They have been used to find all the missing fragments of a crashed aircraft. In hill country mountain rescue teams usually consist of local experts and a number of German Shepherds. The dogs are trained to search for injured climbers in just the same way as the police dogs are trained to search for hidden suspects. Avalanche rescue teams include dogs who will locate people buried under the snow, just as working sheepdogs will locate their buried flocks so that the shepherd may dig them out.

In marked contrast to some of the more aggressive aspects of the German Shepherd's work is the role played by the breed as guide dogs for the blind. The training of dogs to guide the sightless was pioneered on the continent by those anxious to give some mobility to the many men blinded in World War I. Again the reliability and the protectiveness of the German Shepherd meant that it was used more often than any other breed. A number of organizations for training guide dogs were set up in the United States and again German Shepherds were the premier choice. Only in Britain was there an exception as public prejudice plus temperamental difficulties led to the German Shepherd being ousted in the role of guide dog by the Labrador and the Golden Retriever.

Although so widely employed as a working dog the major role of this most versatile of breeds is that of companion. Because this dog is so active in mind and body it needs a responsible owner who takes exercising and training seriously. In return he will find that in the German Shepherd he has reared a dog sensitive to all his moods, protective to his family and a loyal friend for life.

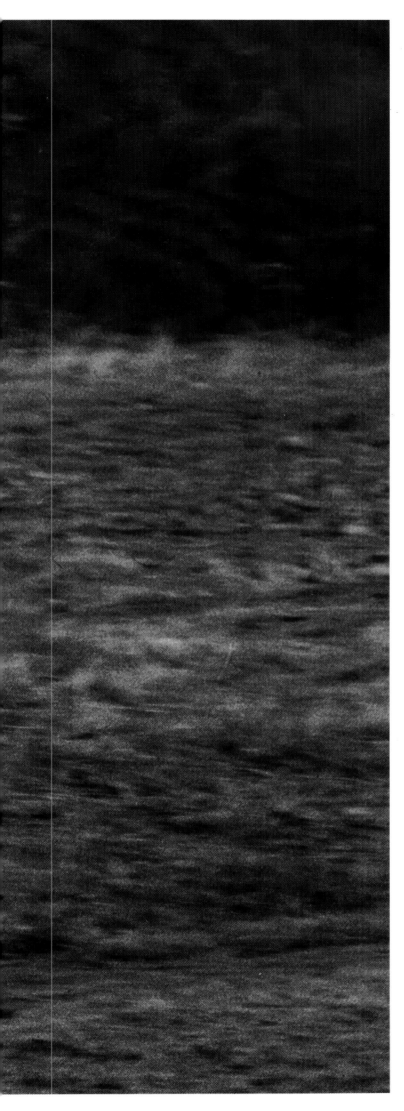

Above: The German Shepherd Dog still fulfils its original role as a sheepdog. A similar dog has probably existed since the days of the caveman but the breed we know today was not evolved until comparatively recently, the first stud books date back only to the end of the nineteenth century. Although all colors are allowed whites, part-whites and creams are not favored today. Black and tan and wolf sable are now the most popular shades for the thick, close-fitting coat.

Left: The German Shepherd has the characteristic slinking gait of the sheepdog which enables it to cover a lot of ground economically. At speed it can easily outrun most men but it is not as fast as the coursing hounds like the Greyhound and Saluki. Sure-footed, and seemingly tireless, it can cover long distances over rough territory without showing strain. If you are prepared to work hard at teaching the dog and learning to control it properly there is no breed that will repay your efforts better, but this is not the dog for anyone of a nervous disposition. Some people keep potentially vicious dogs as a protection against burglars and intruders but without proper control they can be dangerous and the popularity of the breed has led to some dogs of doubtful temperament becoming available.

Collars

The Dog Collar itself has always been more than just a means of restraint. The collar often indicated the status of the dog's owner, even if it did not carry his name and address. It could also tell you what the dog was used for; fighting dogs, coursing dogs, guard dogs, each would wear a different type of collar.

Silver has long been a favorite metal for collars. One of the earliest known was unearthed by archeologists at Pompeii, who uncovered the skeleton of a dog stretched out beside that of a child. The dog had been wearing a silver collar with a Greek inscription saying that his name was "Delta" and that he belonged to Severinus whose life he had saved from a wolf. The earliest travelers through Turkestan saw dogs "the size of asses, and fierce as lions of Africa, which were led along in double chains covered with trappings of rich cloth and wearing silver collars and neckrings."

The German nobility of the seventeenth century valued their mastiffs highly and the best of them wore collars of gold lined with velvet and engraved with their owner's initials. Lesser guard dogs wore silver collars. In the inventory of the belongings of a sixteenth century British king can be found the following items: "... Vi dogge collars of crymson vellat wt. Vi lyhams of white leather. Liame of white silk wt. a collar of white vellat embrawdered wt. perles, with swivel of silver." A lyham, or liame, was a leaf.

The collar could be both an offensive and a defensive weapon and iron collars with spikes on the outside came into use very early. The dog's throat is its most vulnerable area when fighting something like a wolf, so many of the early sheepdogs were equipped with heavy iron-spiked collars. These could be a single hoop of iron with spikes up to four inches long, or a much wider "col en feu", a sort of iron lattice which was studded with one-and-a-half-inch spikes. In some cases a heavy leather collar with sharpened iron nails hammered through it, served instead. Hunting wolves was a sport throughout all the courts in Europe, in some cases the wolfhounds also had protective collars. One which survives consists of a chain of iron links about three inches wide, each link having a couple of protruding spikes.

Whilst the very rich had their collars made of precious metals, and working dogs had iron collars or lengths of rope, dogs belonging to the respectable middle classes very often wore collars made of brass. Brass collars were fashionable through the seventeenth to the nineteenth century and can be seen in many of the oil paintings of this period. The court painter, Sir Godfrey Kneller, was fond of including his patron's canine favorites in his portraits and often put the name of the sitter on the brass band round the dog's neck. The typical brass collar fastened with a slot and staple. A row of three or four slots gave some flexibility of size and a brass padlock through the staple secured the collar. The edges of the collar were usually rolled over so that they did not cut the neck of the dog, and that also gave greater strength to the metal. The whole collar was lined with leather and had a brass ring rivetted on to it through which the lead could be clipped. The owner's name and address might be engraved on the metal, very rarely the date, and hardly ever the dog's name. A variation on this kind of collar had the metal cut into a filigree pattern to allow the colorful leather lining to show through. Some of these collars must have been quite a struggle to put on, as well as uncomfortable to wear, and a few of the smaller ones were hinged in the middle so that they could be opened wide.

Amongst the breeds of dog that wore collars like these were Newfoundlands, Dalmatians, Greyhounds and Poodles, as well as many of the smaller lapdogs. Tiny collars were also made for other pets. An eighteenth century portrait shows a little girl with a pet

Above: A modern Dalmatian wearing the type of brass collar that was fashionable through the eighteenth and nineteenth centuries when these dogs trotted out between the wheels of a gentleman's phaeton. His beribboned colleague is a Yorkshire Terrier.
Right: A Victorian toy dog collar with a row of bells, worn by the smooth variety of Brussels Griffon.

red squirrel wearing a brass collar and chain. Engravings of groups of performing animals show hares and cats wearing similar identification. The collars were often sold by tinkers and by street traders, who also had chains, padlocks and key rings amongst their stock. It has been calculated that in the 1850s in London alone several thousand brass collars were sold annually and it seems very surprising that out of this total so few have survived.

Despite the vogue for brass, Victorian top dogs still went one better. Prince Albert's favorite greyhound, Eos, whose memorial lies at Windsor, wore a silver collar made by a French silversmith. A mock padlock dangles from the collar which opens by a trick mechanism when the "A" of the engraved name "Albert" is pressed. Both London and Parisian jewelers produced expensive trifles to please the owners of expensive dogs. Gold and silver collars could be ordered, both as solid bands or in flexible links. The extravagances did not end there. Parisian poodles wore bracelets of gold and silver and studded with jewels. These locked on to the paw with a padlock in the same way that the metal collars were fastened. In the jewelers' catalogs were leads of gold, couples of gold, even gold or silver muzzles. Possible the ultimate in 1896 was a collar of ivory carved in the shape of a man's dress collar and complete with neat black bow tie and silver bell.

From all this splendor it seems rather a come down to mention leather collars. Nevertheless some of these were very magnificent. The wide leather, brass studded collars worn by fighting dogs emphasise their strength and brutality, rather in the same way that the leather and studs worn by teenage rebels are a declaration of aggression. What are not seen today are the wide collars fringed with badger hair that were worn by early French Bulldogs. It is difficult to understand why this fashion arose: one theory is that the constant tickling encouraged the dog to keep its large ears upright. The wide, soft kid collar shows off the graceful arch of the whippet's neck, while the coursing greyhound wears another specialized collar, a coursing slip, which enables two competing dogs to be loosed at the same moment.

Chain collars are probably in wider use today than they ever were, owing to the popularity of the choke chain as a training collar. At the turn of the century the fashion in chain collars was a series of flat interlocking links, very much on the lines of a horse's curb chain. This too fastened with a padlock and key in the same way as the brass collar it had superseded. The most beautiful of chain collars are those made of such small woven links that they may be likened to fine chain mail.

Most modern dogs wear utilitarian collars and identification tags but it is still possible to buy an off the peg gold collar for your poodle in one of the most famous shops in the world. And, since every chain store sells plastic collars decorated with fake jewels, we may presume that an interest in what your dog wears will never die.

Top: The Pug was a very fashionable lady's pet in the nineteenth century when it might have worn a belled collar like this. Such a collar was often tied at the back of the neck with a ribbon bow and has a felt backing to protect the dog's hair from the rubbing of the chain.

Center: A Pyrenean Mountain Dog wearing the type of spiked collar that would have protected its neck from the jaws of a wolf.

Left: Fighting dogs like these two Staffordshire Bull Terriers wore very impressive, wide collars in metal or leather.

By Sight and Scent

Among the hounds can be found the oldest purebred types of dog and the most beautiful among the many different breeds. The hound group includes two very diverse kinds of animal. One type are the dogs that hunt by sight. They are known by different names in different parts of the world: sighthounds, gazehounds, windhounds or even long dogs. They are all coursing dogs and they use their keen vision to follow their prey, not their sense of smell. They include such breeds as the Greyhound, the Saluki, the Deerhound, the Afghan and the Whippet. Despite differences in size, coloring and coat, these dogs are easily recognizable as being of a related group because of their similarity of shape. Over the centuries they have been bred to be fast. They sight their quarry at a distance and overtake and pull down their prey by sheer superiority of speed. Indeed many gazehounds will lose interest in the chase the minute their adversary goes out of sight. What they cannot see they no longer care about. They have been set to follow such diverse prey as wolves, gazelle, deer and hare, so not only are these dogs agile and swift, they also need to be powerful and courageous.

Physical features which sight hounds share include a narrow, streamlined head with long, powerful jaws. The dog is narrow with an elongated, arched back and a deep chest enclosing a well developed heart and lungs. The animal is muscular with no superfluous body fat. Without sacrificing strength, the legs are long in proportion, and so too is the tail which forms an efficient rudder to an aerodynamically sound body shape. These are the racing dogs, the fastest and fleetest of the dog breeds, with speeds of up to nearly forty miles an hour recorded.

Man no longer courses animals for food and today most of the gazehounds are kept as pets by people who appreciate their symmetry and beauty. On the whole they are gentle dignified animals but the inborn hunting instinct is still just below the surface. A flicker of movement in the distance may well attract the attention of such a dog who will be off to investigate, turning a deaf ear to all commands. Many of these breeds are still coursed by their owners for pleasure. Hares are more often the objects of the chase than anything else, but Deerhounds have been used to course kangaroo in Australia, and in general it may be said of the gazehounds that they need little encouragement to chase anything that runs.

The other section of the hound group have much less in common in their appearance, varying, as they do, from the low-slung Dachshund through the thick-set Elkhound to the lugubrious Bloodhound. However, these are all dogs which follow their quarry by scent and bring it to bay by persistence rather than by sheer speed. The coursing hounds run silently for they need all their breath for their exertions, but the hounds proper bay with excitement when hunting a line and this noise is music to the huntsman's ears. The sounds that the pack makes tell the huntsman a great deal about the scent they are following and how near they are to making a kill.

Obviously, not all kinds of hound live in packs. Bloodhounds, nowadays, are mainly show dogs and pets. Their function as a sporting animal is nearly past. Owners who are worried that the Bloodhound may lose the scenting ability and the perseverance in following a cold trail, for which the breed is justly famous, enter their dogs in working trials. Tracks can be laid of different lengths and duration and the dogs' skill can be tested competitively. In Germany very elaborate trials are held by the Dachshund Club.

A moment of ceremony at the Peterborough Hound Show as huntsman and judge greet each other.

Dachshunds are true hounds with good noses, loud voices and plenty of gameness. The German Club not only tests their ability to track under al sorts of conditions, it also tests the dog's keenness to enter burrows and earths, to bay at the occupants and if possible drive them out. Some of the tests, such as ranging through areas of forest flushing out game and retrieving from water, are similar to those that would normally be expected from the much larger gundogs. The trials are designed to preserve the Dachshund as an allround sporting dog and are not competitive: dogs are graded according to their ability.

Two hounds that thirty years ago were always kenneled in packs have now made the grade as family pets. These are the Beagle and the Basset Hound. Beagles look like pocket sized Foxhounds and have a history going back to the sixteenth century. Beagle packs still hunt the hare and are followed on foot, but the breed today is much better known as a pet and show dog. As with all pack hounds, Beagles are not aggressive towards other dogs, for an aggressive dog would be too disruptive to kennel life. They do, however, tend to have a wanderlust when adult and are independent and stubborn in nature, very valuable qualities when working a difficult line

Above: The Irish Wolfhound, once the valued property of warring Irish kings is usually accepted as the world's tallest dog.

Left: The Borzoi, also known as the Russian Wolfhound was used for wolf coursing by the Czars and Russian nobility. Pairs of dogs, matched in looks as well as speed, were let slip to course a selected quarry.

Right: The Saluki, one of the oldest varieties of purebred dog, was used by desert sheiks for coursing gazelle.

Right: The extraordinary length of the hind limbs of the Afghan Hound gives the leg power to which this breed owes its unrivalled turn of speed across rough ground.

Below: Scottish Deerhounds are a breed that has changed remarkably little in the past 150 years. The use of these hounds for coursing declined with the development of the high-powered rifle but their gentle, dignified bearing ensured that they had enough friends to keep the breed still in existence.

Above: The Afghan really needs a lot of space to be seen at its best. They are dogs built to run freely and they look magnificent when doing so. However, they also tend to be willful and not very obedient, which makes them difficult to exercise in a confined space. Often those which live in towns hardly ever seem to be let off the lead—an unhappy life for so active an animal.

Left: A member of a pack of hunting Basset Hounds waits in a straw-filled kennel. Working Bassets are less cumbersome beasts than show dogs. Their legs are rather longer and straighter and their ears are not quite so long and pendulous. Their heads are much less exaggerated too, without so much loose skin and wrinkle.

The breed originated in France, where the national passion for hunting has been responsible for the evolution of a large number of hound breeds. Bassets barely survived World War I in Britain and then had an enormous surge of popularity as fashionable dogs to own. As they are large energetic dogs on deceptivily short legs, a number of their new owners found that they had more dog than they had bargained for.

41

Above: Dachshunds still retain their original sporting character and, given half a chance, make enthusiastic rabbit hunters. Sadly, they are too often seen waddling on town pavements, overfed and under-exercised. These two are miniatures, a red smooth variety and a black and tan longhair.
Dachshunds come in two sizes, miniature and standard, and three coats, smooth, long-haired and wire. They were originally bred for badger hunting in Germany and possibly come from the same root as the Basset Hound which also has smooth and rough-haired varieties.
Left: A pack of beagles travelling at speed following a scent are not the easiest of dogs to keep up with. Experienced hunt followers often make for the nearest hilltop, confident in the knowledge that the hare will run in a large circle, enabling them to watch most of the hunt from their vantage point.

across country but not always desirable in a pet. The Basset has also become more popular as a pet than as a pack hound. When this first happened, some Bassets did not take kindly to a lonely urban existence, very unlike the warm sociability of pack life enjoyed by their ancestors. A lonely Basset tends to be a noisy Basset and neighborly relations can become strained if a dog howls continuously each time it is left.
The striking appearance of the Foxhound is the result of generations of selective breeding in which function was given greater importance than looks. The result is a beautiful hound standing about twenty four inches high, well-boned, with enormous stamina, and with a peculiarly straight foreleg with tightly knuckled feet. People have attempted to turn the foxhound into a pet as well but this has not been a success. They are dogs of incredible hardness and energy, and this, coupled with a defiance of manner, really only makes them suitable for the discipline of pack and kennel life. The maintenance of a pack of foxhounds is the result of long term planning. Without such forethought the standard of the pack will drop and such faults as exist will become more prevalent. Foxhounds need a good nose to follow a line across all sorts of difficult ground. They need pace and drive to follow hard on the heels of maybe two or three foxes during a hunting day, and they need to give tongue freely when doing so. All these attributes have to be bred for and a certain ruthless selection goes on continually

Above: Few sights are more stirring than a pack of foxhounds streaming across country.

Right: Foxhounds and fox-hunting are found in many parts of the world, transplanted from their British homeland with great success. They make a pretty picture but are really as hard as nails. Centuries of selective breeding have produced a hound which, when fit, can cover fifty miles or more during a hunting day.

Left: Basset Hounds, now popular as pets.

with hounds who are not up to their work being put down or drafted. All the dogs and bitches bred from have proved their ability in the field.

Most foxhound litters are born in the spring and leave the kennels as soon as they are weaned to be reared until they are about a year old by volunteer puppy walkers. Without these people many hunts could not cope and the system ensures that the hound puppies get a certain amount of individual attention and elementary discipline at a time in their lives when they most need it. The young hounds return to the kennels when they are about a year old preferably in the early summer. This enables the huntsman to teach them kennel and pack discipline and to condition them so that they are fit in time for cub-hunting in the autumn. Foxhounds are usually fed at troughs with at watching kennelman to ensure that the slower feeders get their share. The hounds' lives are hard, consisting as they do in the hunting season, of a gruelling day

in the field followed by three or four days rest. Leg, feet and muscle injuries are common and few hounds hunt more than four or five seasons.

The American Foxhound, a slightly different animal, appears in the show-ring as well as the hunting field in the United States. Though it is theoretically possible for an English Foxhound to be shown, in practice it is never done. Instead these hounds have their own shows which are judged in rather a different manner from the usual dog show. Hounds are judged on a leash and running freely about a fenced ring. There is a panel of judges who deliberate and reach a decision without touching the animals at all. Since there are few such Hound Shows, and all the dogs exhibited are primarily kept for hunting, the hounds that appear are always level in type and hard in condition. To a dog show exhibitor they lack the spit and polish that a show dog would automatically receive in a similar situation.

Left: A young wire-haired Dachshund tracking across snow.

Below: The Bloodhound is a sensitive, even shy dog.

Top right: A hound from a beagle pack is judged by quite different methods from those used for show dogs.

Bottom right: French hound breeds are both numerous and very regional.

Chasing the Electric Hare

Greyhound racing is the most popular and money spinning sport connected with dogs. The countries where it is best known are Britain, the United States and Australia. Because of the amounts of money involved in racing, both invested in the tracks and the organization behind them, and also gambled on the races themselves, the sport has always attracted a certain criminal element whose aim was always to shorten the odds in their own favor. For this reason, wherever greyhound racing takes place, it is run by an all powerful ruling body whose aim is to make sure that nothing crooked can possibly occur to interfere with an honestly run race. Whippet racing died because it was known to be a crooked sport where races were rigged so that those in the know could win a great deal with judiciously placed bets. Greyhound racing, to survive, had to live

down this reputation and maintain a clean bill of health. The tightest possible security is kept up on all dogs in training and at all race tracks, making the life of a racing dog one of the most well regulated there is.

Because top dogs can be worth so much and earn their owner's such vast sums of money, a great many people are trying to breed the elusive winner, the record breaker, the money spinner of a lifetime. It is estimated that some ten thousand greyhound puppies are bred in England and Ireland alone each year. Of these perhaps one tenth actually race and a smaller proportion still actually win. Greyhound breeding has always been an Irish industry, there being a certain mystique about an Irish bred greyhound just as there is about an Irish bred horse, a reputation that is not always borne out

Right: The parade before a greyhound race enables the amateur punter to try to pick a winner.

Left: In contrast to the racing dogs these are Italian Greyhounds, the miniature of the greyhound family. They weigh only one tenth of the amount of their larger relatives and have been known and cherished as an elegant and dainty pet since at least the sixteenth century.

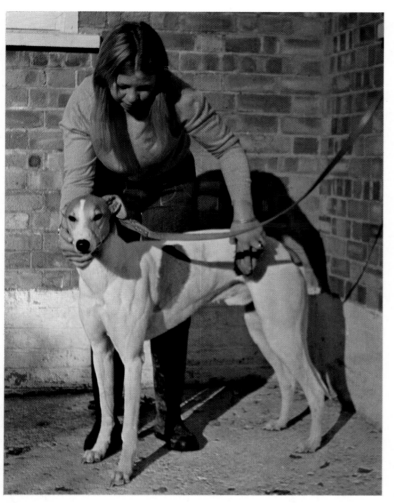

Above: Daily grooming and massaging are routine in racing kennels.
Below: Walking exercise is all part of the conditioning for a racing dog.

by the facts. The old fashioned method of rearing greyhounds was to feed them well and leave them to wander free across the countryside. Now this is no longer possible Irish kennels will run forty or fifty young dogs together in large paddocks until they are old enough to be sent to the sales. This method certainly eliminates the weakest who will be bullied into the ground. Auction sales of young stock are a regular feature. The dogs entered for sale will have run trials giving some indication of their speed, but buying a greyhound at auction is a chancy business even for the experienced.

As fewer people can afford to run on large quantities of dogs in the hope that a small proportion will be good enough, so more greyhounds are sold just after weaning. An owner may wish to run on a pair for himself, but it is no easy matter to pick out the best two in an even litter and a novice buyer stands nearly as good a chance of choosing the best. Most greyhound puppies are well bred. It is not worth breeding from anything that has not done well on the track. When choosing, therefore, buyers should follow the general advice for picking any livestock. Ignore the lethargic and nervous puppy and ignore the whole litter unless they have been well fed and radiate health and energy. Choose the big-boned dog but not the leggy one. The front legs should be long and thick and straight with slight thickening of the joints giving promise of even greater bone to come. The brisket should be deep giving room for heart and lungs. The speed of a running dog comes from back and hindlegs. Longer backed dogs often make better stayers than sprinters, so this is another point to be taken into consideration. What should not influence choice are prejudices against certain colors, slight mouth defects or light eyes. These have no bearing on a dog's racing ability.

Young greyhounds are better kenneled in pairs. In this way they have company and do not get into the bad habits which develop

when larger numbers of dogs are run together. At first the puppies
will get enough exercise playing together in a large enough paddock.
At the age of six months or so the instinct to chase should be
stimulated by giving the youngsters a stuffed rabbit skin to play with.
When this is thrown the rivalry of the dogs to get it and keep it
will ensure they do plenty of twisting and turning as well as the
galloping they need for their muscular development. A refinement
of this is to attach a hare skin to the end of a rod and line. By teasing
the pups with this and then swinging the rod round and paying out
the line the dogs can be encouraged to chase in circles. It is very
important that this is done in both clockwise and anti-clockwise
directions so that the dogs' muscular development is even.
Real schooling for racing begins when a dog is about one year old.
With a young, untrained dog this really consists of two things,
teaching him the mechanics of the race track and conditioning him
so that he is fit enough to run. The race track schooling consists
of introducing the dog to the starting trap. As with race horses
those left at the gate are unlikely to do much winning. A young
greyhound has to learn to leave the trap as if jet propelled, and
to run as close to the rails as it can, for those that run wide at the
bends add a significant number of yards to the distance they have
to run to pass the finishing line. The dog has to get used to wearing
the wire cage type muzzle and the obligatory racing jacket.
The dog will run solo until it has learnt these basic lessons. Only then
will it be introduced to the idea of competing with other dogs.
This is all a preliminary to the animal running in trials. Here its
behavior will be assessed, for any dogs which show tendencies
to snap or play about are automatically debarred from racing.
These trials also give a guide to a dog's speed so that the track trainer
can match dogs of similar standard when drawing up a race card.
The speed of a running dog depends on the length and rapidity

Above: The dogs travel to the stadium under strict security arrangements
to ensure that they cannot be tampered with before a race meeting.
The jockey silks worn by the kennel girls are all part of the showmanship.
Below: Leaving the traps fast is one of the hallmarks of a good dog.

of its stride, and the gait used by greyhounds is similar to that used by nature's fastest sprinters, the cheetah and some of the antelopes such as the pronghorn. This can best be described as a series of extended leaps. The animal pushes off with the hind legs and becomes fully extended in the air with the forelegs stretched out as far as possible in the front. When the forelegs touch the ground, the hindlegs are still in the air and are drawn forward under the body to land in their turn in front of the forelegs, ready for another propulsive effort. The whole is a jack-knife effect depending greatly on the back muscles, which expand and contract like a powerful spring. It is obvious from this that the conditioning of a racing greyhound is the skill which distinguishes the good trainer from the bad. All conditioning starts with walking exercise and dogs

are first introduced to collar and lead at about eight months. The length and pace of the walks are both increased as the animal becomes fitter, and gallops of various lengths are introduced into the training programme. Different programs will be necessary for sprinters and for stayers and the art of a trainer consists of adjusting food and exercise requirements to get the best from each animal. It is impossible to keep a dog in peak condition continually so a racing dog has periods of strict training, alternating with periods of rest when the dog loses a little condition and gains a little weight. Greyhounds can be as temperamental as any other star performers and maintaining a fine edge on the dog's enthusiasm for racing is one of the hallmarks of a good trainer. On the day of a race all competing dogs are checked beforehand

Above: The dog that learns to keep close to the rails has the advantage on the bend.
Left: Over any distance greater than one hundred yards the greyhound is the fastest dog in the world. This bunch are traveling at over thirty miles an hour.
Below: Retired racing greyhounds can make satisfactory pets and there are several organizations devoted to finding good homes for them. This one has found a friend in a Fox Terrier puppy.

by a veterinarian. He looks for obvious signs of illness and lameness and takes a urine sample which will be checked in the laboratory to make sure that the dog has not been drugged. The dogs are then locked up in the care of the race steward. Before the first race those competing have another quick veterinary check up to make sure they are muzzled and jacketed correctly, before being paraded round the track for the benefit of the punters. After each race the dogs are checked again for any injury. Leg, foot and tendon injuries are very common and each stadium retains one or more veterinarians whose concern is two-fold. As well as dealing with injury and illness, they must be ready to detect any dog that has been tampered with to slow it down. Owing to the tight security on most greyhound tracks this is now very rare—but any dog which runs

much above or below its previous known form will be the subject of the closest scrutiny.

Dogs are usually at their best during their second or third racing season and are rarely raced beyond their fourth or fifth. The big winning dogs will be used for breeding but the majority will be put down when their usefulness is ended. There are various organizations engaged in finding homes for retired greyhounds. As all greyhounds with a tendency to fight are eliminated before the start of their racing career, the retired animals are nearly always good with other dogs, although they cannot always be trusted with cats and other small furry creatures. They make gentle, clean, affectionate pets though their spartan lives tends to leave them a little lacking in initiative and personality.

The Wheel of Fashion

Tastes have changed and fashions varied, in dogs as much as in anything else, especially in the toy breeds which were not kept for any utilitarian purpose. These dogs have been the accessories of the society woman throughout history: valued playthings and companions whose presence relieved the tedium of idleness and whose minute size emphasized the feminity of their owners. The graves of ancient Egypt contain the mummified remains of tiny dogs wearing ornate collars, and down through the centuries the portraits of the wives and mistresses of the great show them with small dogs gambolling at their feet or lying on their aristocratic owner's lap, whilst casting an inquisitive glance at the painter. Many of these dogs were toy spaniels of various kinds or the delicate, finely boned Italian Greyhound.

By the nineteenth century the Pug and the Poodle were the fashionable woman's darlings and both were dressed in expensive bits and pieces which were little credit to their owner's sense. There were shops in both London and Paris which specialized in clothing for the pampered toy dog. As well as boots, lingerie and handkerchiefs, you could buy for your pug a yachting costume or a tweed traveling coat with a pocket for its railway ticket. The dog's driving coat, called the Lonsdale, was made to measure of fawn cloth lined with dark red silk. It had a cape collar edged with fur and a frill round the neck finished off with two gold bells. In London, at the same period, an artist with the dog clippers was clipping and shaving fantastic designs on the backs of poodles.

Right: The Afghan Hound is today's fashionable dog, a trendy accessory for the up-to-date man or woman.
Below: The Standard Poodle is the oldest of the three varieties of Poodle and was a very fashionable dog at the end of the last century.

Top: The elegant and aristocratic Doberman Pincher was developed at the end of the last century as a guard dog and is now popular in both Europe and America. Full of fighting spirit and tremendously loyal they need strong handling.
Left: The Bulldog, often used by patriotic Britishers as a national symbol, has come to denote tenacity and solid worth. Originally bred as fighting dogs they can have very gentle personalities, despite their fierce appearance, and can be extremely good with children.
Below: The spotted coat of the Dalmatian added a final touch of distinction to a gentleman's turnout in the nineteenth century. Most of the dogs were expected to trot between the rear wheels of his carriage but in some cases they were encouraged to station themselves under the pole between the pair of horses.

Dogs of titled owners had their master's crests or monograms silhouetted by the clippers. Any sort of pattern or set scene could be ordered and as the dog had to return monthly to have the design retrimmed, the man with the clippers had an assured income. Apparently, before one big race, this master craftsman clipped the outline of a racehorse on one of his own poodles, leaving an untrimmed patch on which he cut the name of the winning horse as soon as it became known. He then sought out the owner, who was celebrating his win, and sold the dog to him for a large sum. Poodles again became one of the most fashionable breeds to own in the 1960s. This time though it was the Miniature Poodle, a smaller version of the Standard Poodle which had been the rage in the 1890s. This clever and vivacious dog seems to lend itself to the extravagances of fashion and the popularity of the breed once again led to a great increase in the numbers of dog beauty parlors

and dog accessories. The modern dog has been saved the indignity of having pictures shaved on the hair of its back, but the coat can still be clipped in any number of different ways, of which the Lion and the Dutch clips are the most popular. It is not unknown for the modern Poodle to be dyed to match its owner's outfit or for its toenails to be painted the same shade as its mistress's fingernails.

The Rough Collie is another breed which has enjoyed two periods of great popularity. At the turn of the century it was the fashionable breed to own and very high prices were paid for good show collies. There was another great increase in their numbers thirty years later when a series of sentimental novels with a collie hero became best-sellers and the film "Lassie Come Home" was made. This is not the only time that a film has boosted the numbers of a breed for Dalmatians benefited when Disney made a cartoon featuring them. The reasons for a breed becoming popular are mostly guesswork but certainly it needs to be distinctive enough to be easily recognizable by the layman. Sometimes it is a spin-off from advertising that brings a breed to the public's notice. Currently both Old English Sheepdogs and Basset Hounds are enjoying a boom due to both breeds being used in world wide advertising campaigns. The Bulldog is another breed which has enjoyed steady popularity partly due to it being continually before the public eye as a national symbol. Publicity, of course, works both ways and the slump in the numbers of German Shepherds in the 1930s was directly attributable to the bad press they received after a number of tragedies when rogue individuals of the breed attacked various people. Eminent owners do a great deal for breed publicity too. It was the interest of Queen Victoria in the Rough Collie which helped to make it popular, just as the present British Queen's in the Welsh Corgi has increased that dog's numbers. Fashion photographs and film stars publicity shots have often included a stylish and expensive dog to increase the atmosphere of luxury and elegance. Fifty years ago the pretty girl had a couple of Borzois straining at the leash, a fox fur over one shoulder and the bonnet of a Lagonda in the background. Today's model had very much the same type of dog, only now it is the currently popular Afghan Hound. The Wire Fox Terrier, and the Cocker Spaniel, followed by the Poodle, have all become world wide favorites in their time. The current favorite is probably the German Shepherd but it is by no means an out and out leader for both the Labrador Retriever and the diminutive Yorkshire Terrier are nearly as strong numerically. There is only one certainty about the future and that is that the current favorite will be dethroned. Not only is fashion fickle but every breed that becomes very popular attracts the unscrupulous who want to make money out of it. Where a large number of puppies are turned out solely with the idea of a quick profit, quality in both health and temperament decline. These are the two essentials for the family pet and when a breed declines on both counts the public turn elsewhere.

Above: The Borzoi, an aristocrat among breeds, has always been a status symbol as much as a pet. It was particularly popular in the 1920s and was included in a number of art deco pottery and sculpture groups.
Developed for the rather stylized and artificial sport of wolf coursing by the Russian nobility, their usefulness came to an abrupt end with the success of the October Revolution. Fortunately by that date they had already become established in America and Western Europe.
Big and beautiful, they exude good breeding—but they do need owners who have the time and money to afford their upkeep.
Left: Very large breeds have always been kept as status symbols. Dogs like these Great Danes need plenty of space and a great deal to eat.
Right: Gundogs are often used in advertising to suggest the appeal of the outdoor life and an air of relaxed manliness. The two are Gordon Setters.

The Herdsman's Partner

Man and dog are believed to have associated first as hunters. The dog was the first animal domesticated and used by man and remains his most versatile servant. Possibly it is this long acquaintanceship which has made the dog so responsive to man's needs and so willing to be used in such diverse ways. The second animal domesticated and used by man was probably the reindeer and, from being a hunter, the dog was adapted to being a herding and guarding animal. By the time that the domesticated dog reached Europe, which was well over four thousand years ago, it was already a general purpose animal ready to guard his master's belongings and his herds from thieves and predators alike. There is reason to believe that such animals resembled the general utility, spitz type breeds which still perform the same functions on Scandinavian farms today. There are some seventy breeds of sheepdogs and herding dogs in the world today but many of these no longer work for their living. Cattle which used to travel on the hoof, from the grazing grounds to market or slaughterhouse, now go by road or rail. The beasts arrive in much better condition and the dogs which used to escort them, often for hundreds of miles, are no longer needed. Breeds like Rottweilers and Welsh Corgis, both cattle dogs, have to find new roles, as police dogs, or show dogs, or companions. Some breeds, like the Lancashire Heeler, simply disappear for ever. Many dogs, which people think of as sheepdogs are no longer capable of doing the work for which they were originally bred. Amongst these are the Rough Collie, the Shetland Sheepdog, the Smooth Collie and the Old English Sheepdog. Some other breeds are in a transitional stage being used for work in their country of origin and only being known as show dogs elsewhere. Dogs in this category include such animals as the Komonder, Puli, Maremma and Anatolian Karabash.

The real workers of the sheepdog world vary a great deal in size and looks and perform a number of different functions. The common factor amongst them is that most of their behavior is instinctive. It has been bred into them for generation after generation. The only form of selection used was whether the dog was able to work, the look of the animal being of very secondary importance. The training that working sheepdogs receive merely brings out and controls what are inherent characteristics.

In some parts of the world the function of a sheepdog is still that of a guard against animals such as wolves. Obviously dogs like this have to be large and powerful. They sometimes wore spiked collars which served not only to protect the vulnerable throat area but also as offensive weapons when they were attacking and driving off marauders. Many such dogs had their ears cropped in the belief that it made them fiercer. Cropped sheepdogs normally have the whole tip of the ear removed, making a broad head look even more powerful and wider. It is possible that, since the ear bleeds freely, the custom arose to remove as much of the ear flap as possible giving opponents little chance to grip it. Certainly superstition also plays a part as in some parts of the world the ear tips were fed back to the dog in the belief that this would make the animal stronger. Most of these guard dogs were left to look after the flocks at night. They were expected to act on their own initiative and they needed to have plenty of courage and independence of spirit. Breeds like the Maremma, mainly used to guard folded flocks at night in Central Italy, and the Pyrenean, which used to be a protection against wolves, are dogs of character needing a fair amount of training.

Other sheepdogs, smaller in build and less specialized in type, are used as watchdogs rather than guards. These are more common where it is the custom to keep nomadic herds of both sheep and goats in areas of poor grazing where large predators are few. These dogs travel with the shepherds and the flocks, helping to round up the stragglers, separating the milking ewes and generally giving warning of the odd and the unusual which might be potential dangers. Nomadic flocks tend to be steadier than sheep who see man but rarely. They are very often led by an old ewe distinguished by a bell hung round her neck. Where their leader goes the flock will follow and for this reason the sheepdogs with these flocks do not need to be the sophisticated workers found in other parts of the world.

Obviously local farming conditions dictate the kind of work needed from the sheepdogs in that particular country. Where fencing is too expensive to be practical, the dogs may be required to spend their entire time keeping the sheep out of the crops. This type of work was one of the things required of the German Shepherds and of the Belgian Sheepdogs. Such dogs were not able to produce sudden short bursts of speed but required an effortless, tireless lope that covered ground in the most economical manner as they spent their time continually rounding up stragglers and breakaways from the main flock. Where large flocks under different ownership grazed side by side, the sheepdogs were expected to keep the respective flocks apart and sort out the strays. A variation on this type of work was when the railway companies in Wales employed sheepdogs to keep the unfenced railway lines clear of sheep. Where sheep graze mountainous country, living semi-wild for most of the year and only being gathered in for dipping or culling, dogs are the only means of gathering together flocks spread so far over much difficult terrain. Often these were noisy workers, very different from the silent stealthy trials dog. A breed such as the Scottish Bearded Collie would be sent out to the upper limit of the grazing area, often far out of sight of the shepherd, and would there start moving the sheep downhill by sweeping backwards and forwards across the mountainside keeping up a continuous barking. The noise has the effect of frightening sheep hidden from the dog

All sheepdog breeds are marked by sensitivity and a desire to please. It is as though their close association with man has made them extra responsive to our moods. Like this sheepdog with his master on the island of Cyprus there are countless working dogs that have been evolved locally and do not fit any strict breed specification.

in ravines and gullies and getting them on their feet and moving downhill towards the shepherds in the valley. Early settlers took the Bearded Collie to Australia and New Zealand. It did not survive in the former country mainly because it was too heavily coated for the climate. However in New Zealand the Bearded Collie adapted well to the mountainous regions of the South Island and gave rise to a dog now known as the New Zealand Huntaway. This dog is a specialized sheepdog used to drive sheep out of the rough and mountainous areas. Trials are held for huntaways to assess the most valued attributes, those of noise, style of working and response to command.

Australia has two types of working sheepdog, the native Kelpie and the ubiquitous Border Collie. The Kelpie is one of the finest working breeds and one that in its homeland is also popular with show-goers. It is a highly valued dog with a great deal of interest taken in its working ability as assessed by trials. Both the press and the public in Australia hold the dog in great esteem. The Kelpie has been purebred for about a century. Theories about its origin are nebulous but it is assumed that Scottish and Welsh sheepdog stock, and the native Australian Dingo, played a part in creating the breed. The modern dog is a compact, square, smooth-coated animal with a wedge shaped head and upright ears. There is a great impression of alertness and initiative. Though powerful and muscular, with a deep and roomy ribcage, the dog is still very lithe and flexible in its movement. The breed has, and needs, great endurance as the distances over which it works sheep are very great. It is also better able to withstand heat than many of the other working

Above left: A Border Collie gathers up a flock of sheep. Border Collies vary considerably in type. In general they are medium sized dogs, rather long in the back and very lithe and supple in their movements. The coat is thick and waterproof but can vary in length, and is never so heavy as in some of the continental sheepdogs.

Left: Two champion Bearded Collies— but show dogs not working ones. This is a breed which is in the transitional stage of turning from a working animal into a dog which is kept mainly as a pet. The heavy coat is waterproof enough to keep the dog's skin dry even when it has been swimming. Shepherds never groomed these sheepdogs but the Beardie was often shorn and dipped with the sheep as a way of keeping their coats in order.

Above: One of the more serious faults in a working dog is to grip or bite the sheep. This would disqualify a trial dog. In many Australian sale yards it is usual for dogs to have their canine teeth removed to restrict damage to the sheep. When a dog is traveling at speed the impulse to bite must be very great. However the ideal sheepdog has a quiet forcefulness when dealing with the flock.

Right: Farm Collies like this one are accustomed to fitting in anywhere that they are likely to be needed.

Above: The working type Bearded Collie tends to be lightweight compared with its show counterpart. This could be because the working dog gets a great deal more exercise and is often expected to do a day's work before it is fully mature.

Right: Vast distances and poor grazing are typical of much sheep rearing country. They make for hard and thirsty work for shepherd and dogs.

Below: The blue merle Rough Collie is now far removed from its working ancestors: their broad skull has been refined to a narrow snipey head, it carries much more coat and has lost the swinging economical lope of the working animal.

sheepdogs. Black and tan or red are the most popular colors, but blue, chocolate and fawn are also quite common.

Australian sheep husbandry involves very large distances and very large numbers of animals. A single Kelpie accompanying a stockman on horseback can do the work of a dozen men. Gathering and moving big mobs of sheep is only one aspect of a Kelpie's work. Some dogs are encouraged to be lead dogs. These keep ahead of the sheep, steadying the pace of the flock to suit the speed of those at the tail end. Such dogs will block off crossroads or side turnings if the sheep are being moved on a road, and will turn the sheep on command if they are moving across country. Some dogs will work the wings of a big flock of sheep keeping in the stragglers, particularly important when the flock is strung out approaching water.

Right: An Australian kelpie team hold a sheep and her lamb with their skill.

Far right: The Briard is a French sheepdog with a very long history of working both sheep and cattle. Like many other of the larger sheepdog breeds it has distinguished itself in other fields, notably as an army dog in World War I. It is also now working with a number of continental police forces. Both in the United States and Britain the Briard is known as a show dog.

Below: The instinct of a sheepdog is to go out and gather together almost any moving animal. This Border Collie is working a small flock of ducks and saving someone getting wet feet. Some farmers teach their dogs the basic words of command while making them work ducks. Only when the dogs understand what is required of them are they taken out with the sheep.

Bottom right: It is a common belief when training sheepdogs that a young animal will benefit by running with and copying an older, more experienced dog but this is not necessarily the case, the youngster being able to pick up as many bad habits as good. However it does save time and is a short cut often employed. These are Border Collies, the most widespread of working sheepdogs.

The driving dogs behind the mob have to be forceful enough
to move on frightened or reluctant sheep without ever being tempted
to bite and hang on. In common with sheepwork in other parts
of the world the Kelpie too has to be taught to hold a flock together
in one place for as long as is necessary for shearing or other needs.
In the big Australian sale yards, there are further specialized
workers. Some dogs are encouraged to become noisemakers whose
barking will help keep the sheep moving. Some dogs become expert
at emptying the sheep-filled railway trucks coming into the sale yards.
Others are taught to run across the backs of the tightly packed sheep
in order to get to the leaders and keep them moving in the right
direction. When so much depends on the dog, it is not surprising
that so much care goes into their breeding and training.
The most wide-spread and well-known of the world's working
sheepdogs is the Border Collie. There is some controversy over
the name as some people feel the title working sheepdog would be
more appropriate for an animal which shows such a wide variation
in type and appearance. The "border" referred to in the name
is that between England and Scotland where there have always been
many fine working collies. The sagacity of these hill collies
caught public fancy in the nineteenth century. Helped by the fact
that Queen Victoria owned and liked the collie, it became very
fashionable to own and then to show them. The collie was improved.
The dog was bred larger, the muzzle much snipier, the coat
much longer, so that the name Rough Collie became appropriate.
Meanwhile the working collie remained, smaller, lighter and
rather less distinguished in appearance doing the job for which

it was intended. The Border Collie spread throughout the British Isles ousting or absorbing many of the local sheepdogs. Bred solely for its working ability the fame of the Border Collie was carried around the world and they are known and respected wherever sheep are farmed. As working dogs they are used in the United States of America and in Australia they are not only a mainstay of the work force but are also recognized in the show ring. Border Collies have been exported widely. Some of the earliest accounts of trading between European countries show that trained dogs were a valuable commodity, and this is still true today, as far as the Border Collie is concerned.

The qualities that make the breed so pre-eminent as a working animal have been fixed by many generations of selective breeding. The most obvious instinct that the dog needs to possess is the herding instinct. This is not apparent in young puppies and may not show until the dog is a year old or more. The desire "to run"— to go out and gather up sheep or indeed anything else that moves— cannot be taught. It is something that is bred into the working animal. One of the reasons why a well bred Border Collie puppy is valued, even though its herding instinct cannot be assessed, is the fact that its parents were known to possess this instinct and the puppy can therefore be expected to have inherited it. This herding instinct must be coupled with an equally strong desire to obey, otherwise the dog will simply run riot and prove untrainable. Intelligence and initiative are also very valuable qualities particularly in the general purpose farm dog who often has to cope with a situation on its own without commands from an omnipresent master. However these two qualities are easier to pick out at a younger age in any litter of puppies. The ringleaders where mischief and exploration are concerned are usually those with the most intelligence.

Far left: A working sheepdog of the Caucasus. Such a powerfully built dog will be used more as a guard than as a herding animal.

Left: A French shepherd and his dog. France has produced a number of sheepdog breeds, all of them robust, reliable workers.

Bottom, far left: Old English Sheepdogs line up for the judges at a show.

Bottom left: The Komondor, sheepdog of the Hungarian steppes, is a very old and well established breed which lives a semi-nomadic existence in its native land, looking after flocks of very active, long-legged sheep. This is one of the largest of the actively working sheepdogs, males being more than twenty-five inches at the shoulder. The extraordinary coat takes many years to develop fully. The entire body is covered with long, soft, woolly white hair which after years of exposure to wind and rain felts and mats into a solid fleece which drags on to the ground. Even though they are strong and exceptionally active dogs, it seems strange that this weight of coat does not impede them in their work. The Komondor is now being shown in both Britain and the United States. In Hungary the show dog is exhibited with the coat twisted into long strands.

The pre-eminence of the Border or Working Collie as the world's foremost sheepdog must be due in part to the institution of sheepdog trials and later to the founding of the International Sheepdog Society. The first trials were held in Wales in 1873 and were instantly successful. Since then the idea of sheepdog trials of one kind or another has spread all over the pastoral world. Measuring the working ability of dogs by well-organized competitive tests is a sure way of raising the level of achievement by both trainers

Right: Dogs marked heavily with white often have one brown and one blue eye. The blue, or wall eye is also often associated with a merle coat. There is a long held superstition amongst shepherds that a blue eye focuses better on distant objects and a brown eye sees better at close range. Odd-eyed dogs are supposed to enjoy the advantages of both types of vision.
Below: The Tervueren is one of three closely allied Belgian sheepdog breeds. All were originally herding dogs and guards but are now more usually trained for police and obedience work.
Below center: Working sheepdogs do not always make satisfactory pets. The desire to work is so strong that, when it is frustrated, nervous tension makes the animal neurotic. Such dogs are happier when given something to do. It doesn't matter whether that be learning tricks—like this working collie going down a children's slide—or more serious fields of competitive work and obedience training, your dog will be happier and more of a companion.
Bottom right: Border Collies bring sheep down from the hills.

and animals. Although it can be said that many trials-winning sheepdogs would be little use on the average farm, as they are trained to work almost exclusively to command and have little chance to use their initiative to solve problems, nevertheless the success of the trials winning dog is due to inherent instincts necessary for all sheepdogs and their progeny are therefore almost all likely to be competent workers.

Sheepdog Trials are held at all levels from the small local event to International meetings. The dogs at each meeting all complete the same course which is designed to demonstrate their skill in gathering and driving sheep and their ability to negotiate a flock through obstacles such as gates. The dogs must be able to select out such sheep as are indicated to them and keep them under control, a process known as "shedding". Finally the sheep must be penned. There is a time limit on the course and each exercise has a scale of points, though much leeway is given to the judge's discretion. The International Sheepdog Society was founded in 1906 and now organizes the major sheepdog trials in the British Isles. Possibly more important is its institution of a Stud Book which registers only those working collies whose abilities have been proved, and their progeny. Being in the International Sheepdog Society's Stud Book is therefore a guarantee that the dog will have the right inherent qualities to make a worker.

Contrasts and Comparisons

The world's dog breeders have produced countless different varieties of dog to carry out particular duties or to suit an individual whim. There are more than three hundred and forty different breeds recognized in various parts of the world today, although not all of them will be acceptable to canine bodies in every country.

The tallest dog is generally considered to be the Irish Wolfhound, which measures about three feet at the shoulder, and the smallest is the Chihuahua with an average weight of between two and four pounds.

Left: The Old English Mastiff has a long tradition of fighting behind it but today's animals are gentle giants compared with those of the past.

Right: The alert and dainty Papillon.

Below: The massive Saint Bernard and a little long-haired Chihuahua.

Top: The elongated Borzoi head.
Top centre: The giant-sized Great Dane. A strong muscular dog which is this big needs to be good natured and well behaved or it can become a menace.
Above: The diminutive Affenpinscher.
Right: The Hungarian Puli has more coat than anything else, the mature dog being so well covered that it is difficult to distinguish one end from the other. The coat is usually "corded," that is, twisted into long ropes.

Left: The long-haired variety of the little Chihuahua.
Below: The long-nosed Afghan, with its luxuriant coat.
Below left: Chinese Crested Dogs. Hairless dogs have always had great curiosity value but little is known about their origin.
Bottom left: A smooth-coated Chihuahua puppy, a very popular breed.
Bottom below: The flat-faced Pekingese, a demanding and temperamental dog despite its small scale.

The Sportsman's Companion

Many of the gundog breeds are extremely popular as pets and are better known as family dogs than they are working in the shooting field. One of the reasons why so many of them make such good family pets is their reliable and kindly temperament. They are dogs that have been bred for a willingness to please, for it is on this factor that all training is based, and the gundog, to be of any use, must be an obedient dog. Another of the more delightful characteristics of the gundog is an enthusiastic participation in man's enjoyments. This, in the working dog, is what develops into a passion for the job which keeps the dog going through thick, thorny undergrowth, icy water and a dozen other natural hazards met with in a long shooting day. It therefore follows that most gundogs have plenty of energy and need adequate space and time spent on exercising. They are also dogs that have been selected for generations for a natural interest in fur and feather, so their curiosity about next door's poultry or the neighborhood cats shoud be kept under control.

Compared with the coursing dogs and the scent hounds, the gundog breeds are of very recent origin. Before the gun came into use as a sporting weapon, there was no need for them, and their subsequent history has been closely allied with developments in the sport of shooting. Gundogs can be roughly divided into four groups whose work with the gun is slightly different. The oldest of these groups are the spaniels which have certainly been working as sporting dogs since the fourteenth century, and were helping the capture of game birds long before shooting was possible. This was also long before there were different breeds of spaniel, although there may well have been different types preferred for different kinds of country and different sorts of game. Breeds subsequently take shape from these regional and local distinctions but usually this is a matter of gradual evolution rather than set purpose and, in the case of the spaniel, did not take place until at least four hundred years after they are first mentioned as sporting dogs.

Before considering what the spaniel did then as opposed to what it does now, something else should be borne in mind and that is the fact that shooting at flying birds was not really a practicable proposition much before 1700. Before then the only way to kill birds on the wing was to employ falcons, and falconry, of course, was an extremely popular sport. Most game birds were captured on the ground when they were feeding or in hiding and spaniels were employed in various ways to help.

One method was for the dogs to drive the game towards strategically placed nets and traps, something very akin to the flushing of game from the undergrowth which spaniels are still expected to do. A fifteenth-century writer describes how the spaniels went ahead of their masters with their tails wagging all the time—a typical spaniel trait! Other spaniels were employed in capturing duck, either fledglings too young to fly or adults deep in moult. The most interesting way of capturing birds with the help of spaniels

Above: The Springer Spaniel is a well balanced dog, robust and strong in build. It would seem to be the ideal countryman's companion, able and willing to join in with anything that is suggested.
Left: The soft freckles of color on a white silky background make the coat of the English Setter one of its chief glories. This dog, whose job is to find and point game, is amongst the most popular of bird dogs with the American sportsman. In its country of origin the breed is kept mainly as a pet. The color of these dogs is described as orange belton, that is, orange and white. The American standard also lists tricolor, blue belton, lemon belton and liver beton as permissible colors.

was a method of netting. The dogs located a covey or even a nesting bird and, approaching as close as they dare without flushing the birds, the spaniels then crouched down indicating where the birds were to the hunters with them. The men then flung a net over both the birds and the dogs. Because of the way the dogs crouched, they were said to "sitt" or "sett" and were sometimes called "setting Spanniells".

Shortly after this spaniels did divide into two kinds, the land spaniels and the water spaniels, who were used on windfowl. It is from water dogs like the latter that such modern breeds as the Portuguese

Water Dog, the Pont-Audemer Spaniel and the Irish and American Water Spaniels may have come.

By 1800 the land spaniels were of two different types. The larger of the two was called the Springer whose job it was to find and spring the game, for by now it was possible to shoot birds in flight rather than on the ground. The other was called a Cocker and was a smaller dog able to work the thick undergrowth frequented by woodcock. The nineteenth century was the heyday of the shooting dog and the nine or ten separate spaniel breeds were evolved during this period. All of them did much the same work, searching for

Right: The Curly Coated Retriever was a favorite of nineteenth century sportsmen. It is a strong, keen working dog but the caprice of fashion has led to a decline in numbers.
Below: Pointers were bred to gallop freely across the moors, endlessly quartering the ground for game. They gallop with the head up, scenting the air, unlike the hound which puts its nose to the ground. These elegant, racy dogs are not really suited to town life.

and pushing out game for the guns to shoot, and then finding the dead or wounded animals and bringing them back to the sportsman Increasing urbanization in the twentieth century has meant a decline of shooting in the grand manner and some of the spaniel breeds have declined with it. The Sussex, Field, Clumber and Irish Water Spaniels are all few in number and kept in existence by small bands of dedicated enthusiasts. Other spaniels, like the Cocker, have successfully taken the step from field to hearth and are now pet and show dogs with little pretence at working ability. The two breeds which are still pre-eminent in the field are the English Springer and the Brittany Spaniel. The Springer is an excellent all purpose dog for the modern shooting man and is also well known as a pet and a show dog. There is however a distinct difference in type between the show and the working dog. The Brittany Spaniel is widely known and used on the continent and is one of the most popular bird dogs in America. This is the only "pointing" spaniel and again is an excellent all-round gundog. Great efforts have been made by the American Club looking after the breed's interests to prevent the split, which so often occurs in gundog breeds, where the working dogs and the show dogs

Left: The shooting dog is a seasoned traveler. A black and white Springer Spaniel looks out from the back of his master's automobile. Liver and white is the more usual color for this breed.
Below: A gamekeeper with a pair of yellow Labradors. Popular as domestic pets, Labradors are also one of the most popular retrievers among working dogs and are also used as guide dogs for the blind.

begin to develop markedly different in looks and ability.

The classic dog amongst the pointers is the English Pointer. This is descended from the old Spanish Pointer, a slow heavy breed whose instinctive habit of freezing into a trance like pose when scenting game fascinated and astonished early travelers. The Spanish Pointer is no longer in existence but the breed is behind a large number of continental bird dog breeds and was also the cornerstone of the English Pointer. When the Spanish dog was first imported into Britain its slow, cautious working admirably suited a sportsman burdened with a cumbersome firearm, who needed time to adjust the charge and make various other arrangements before the gun would fire. As guns improved so did the dog. Efforts were made to increase the dog's speed and various crosses were tried, notably with a Foxhound. This led to a faster animal without any loss of scenting powers. However as pointers use air scent to locate their birds and foxhounds follow a scent with their noses to the ground, some loss of style was also a result, and a lot of time was spent by dog trainers in the early 1800s devising methods of keeping their pointer's heads up when they were searching for birds. Pointers in Britain were mainly used to quarter the moors to find grouse. They were bred to cover a lot of ground at a gallop, always

A pair of Wire-haired German Pointers and their masters prepare to set off for a day's sport in the Frankfurter woods. It is a versatile dog and its water-repellent coat makes it particularly suited to hunting waterfowl.

searching for that elusive air scent which would freeze them into a trancelike point indicating to the sportsman where the birds were hidden. With the break up of more and more of the big grouse moors in Britain the numbers of working pointers have become minimal and the breed is mainly found in the show ring. The only country with space enough to work English Pointers in the style for which they were bred, is America.

The Spanish Pointer spread from its original home into Germany, France and Russia. In each of these countries it was crossed with native breeds and is thus behind most of the continental pointers and setters. The best known of these such as the Weimaraner, the German Short-haired Pointer and the Vizsla, are all dual purpose gundogs. They are expected to find and point game, remain steady to shot, and find and retrieve the dead and wounded birds. This means that they are more likely to be adaptable to changing conditions in the shooting field and can be expected to have some sort of working future.

It seems very likely that the setter breeds came from the crossing of the "setting Spanniells" with the Spanish Pointer, perhaps in an effort to get some of the typical spaniel bustle into the stolid Pointer stock. The original purpose of the setter was similar to that of the pointer. They were required to quarter the ground ahead of the sportsman to find the game. When they scented their bird they indicated its presence by standing rigidly with head outstretched, frozen into immobility until the hunter flushed and shot the bird.

Again the only country left with space enough to work setters in any numbers is America. However, as the three main setter breeds are very striking in appearance, they have attracted a large number of admirers who are happy to keep them as pets. The happy-go-lucky Irish Setter is a deep mahogany red in color with a gleaming silky coat that attracts attention wherever he goes. The breed tends to be scatterbrained, energetic and affectionate in nature, whilst the English Setter is a little more placid and sentimental. Instead of the flashy red of the Irish Setter, the English counterpart has a silky white coat freckled and splotched with pastel shades

Left: The Weimaraner, originally produced in Germany, is now found in its greatest numbers in the United States. American sportsmen appreciated its all round utility as a gundog and it is popular as a field trial competitor. The all silver or mouse gray color has earned them the nickname "ghost dogs."
Below: Two liver and white gundogs, both English breeds: the smooth-coated English Pointer and the English Springer Spaniel.

of blue, orange or lemon. The third of the group comes from Scotland and is the least known, though the black and tan coloring of the Gordon Setter is also very striking. This is a more heavily built dog than the other two with a good nose and plenty of perseverance in the field.

The last group of the gundogs, and historically the most recent, are the retrievers. The name first of all merely denoted the use to which the dogs were put, and anything and everything in the way of a dog taken out by the sportsman to collect for him any game that he shot. Pointers and Setters were expected to retrieve,

and in some parts of the world still are, but otherwise almost anything was pressed into service. We are told of terrier-beagle crosses and even crossbred Bloodhounds who were all used and called retrievers. From the success that the later retriever breeds had in the field, we may deduce that these early dogs were not too good at the job of discovering wounded game and recovering dead birds that had fallen into places where they were not easily found.

Three of the four retriever breeds, the Curly-coat, the Flat-coat and the Labrador, all come from the same root stock, an active, black, water-loving dog from Newfoundland. Of the three,

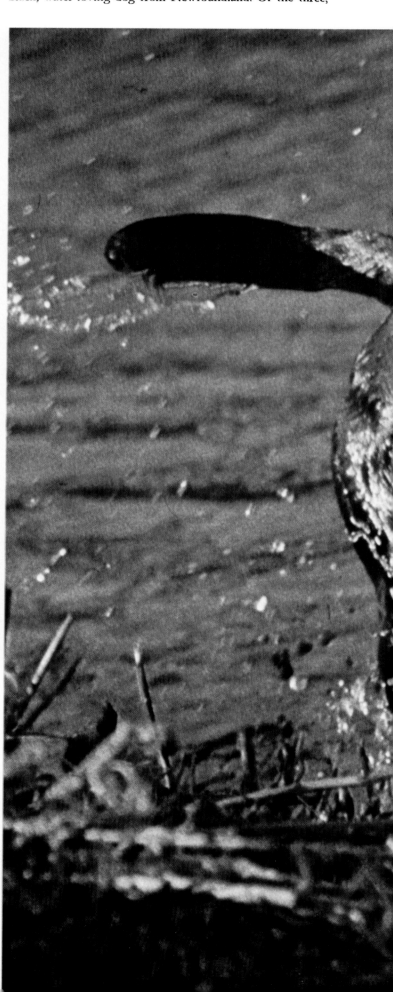

Above: Breeds such as this Irish Water Spaniel are particularly good at retrieving from water and make the ideal choice of gundog for the wildfowler. They are good swimmers and impervious to cold but, like many Irish breeds, they are tough and headstrong. The tight, crisp curls of the coat are waterproof and oily, and smell quite pungent when they are wet, which is one possible reason why the breed has never been widely kept as a pet. They are a dog with a clownish sense of humor.

Right: A black Labrador Retriever fetches its bird back. Although the coat of the dog is dripping wet on the outside the skin will still be dry as the hair acts as an efficient insulator against both cold and wet.

the Labrador is by far the most popular today although, as with the pointer and the setter, the use of the retriever in the shooting field has declined. However the Labrador, together with the fourth member of the group, the Golden Retriever, is a very versatile dog. Both these breeds are immensely popular family dogs, being even-tempered, biddable animals. Moreover the Labrador is used widely as a police dog, in particular where nosework is required and large numbers of both breeds are trained as guide dogs for the blind.

The future for some of the gundog breeds seems rather uncertain.

The all-round working gundogs, such as the Springer Spaniels and the eminently practical continental pointing breeds, will survive because they are suitable for today's conditons in the shooting field and their usefulness to the sportsman will continue. Equally, those breeds which, like the Cocker Spaniel, have become popular as pets and for whom any pretence at continued working ability has been abandoned, will also be assured of their place by the fireside. But, on the other hand, some of the more esoteric gundog breeds, which have not become known in other fields, seem unlikely to be able to continue for very much longer.

The Family Pet

Since the first puppies of the domesticated dog played with the children of prehistoric man by the fire at the mouth of their cave home the dog has been a family pet. No other animal so readily joins in every day-to-day activity, defends the home and family property as his and gives that unquestioning loyalty that only family duties and the ties of blood produce in man.

Often a dog will show particular devotion to one member of the family but it will want to be an acknowledged part of the whole household. Like other members of the family it may show jealousy at attention given to a new arrival but unlike us it will rarely bear a grudge for long and it will always try to please. We cannot chose our relations, but we can chose our dogs— or chose not to have a dog at all. When you buy a dog you really do add another member to your family so it is not a step to be lightly undertaken but deserves considerable thought. For all the pleasure it will bring it will also be a great responsibility and sometimes a thorough nuisance. When you plan holidays, visits

or even nights out you will have to arrange for it to be fed and cared for, or take it with you, and the person whom it acknowledges as master will not necessarily be the one who has to spend time looking after it.

The animal is going to have to be the responsibility of one of the adult members of the family, in practice usually the wife of the partnership, not only through the fluffy, adorable baby stage, but also through the gangling, chewing, awkward adolescent stage, and

Right: One of the pleasures of owning a pedigree animal is that it is possible to chose a breed which is likely to suit the temperament or that pleases the eye. With so many breeds to chose from there is something to please everyone. These distinguished looking dogs, so very much part of the household, are Gordon Setters.
Below: The Keeshond, or Dutch Barge Dog, actually originated in Germany but they became the symbol of the Dutch spirit and a favorite companion for bargemen. From the Netherlands they were taken to England where this one was photographed on a Thames barge.

day after day for the next ten years or more. It is inevitably going to leave mud on the floor, hairs on your clothes and be sick in the middle of the carpet. It may well commit other crimes like chewing the Chippendale, or digging up the rose bushes. It also has a number of needs some of which can be expensive and some of which can be inconvenient. A dog must have a relatively high protein diet which, with an animal of any size, will be expensive to provide. It needs daily exercise whatever the weather and however you feel. In this automobile age the days have long since passed when any dog could be let out to go for a walk by itself. Furthermore a dog is a sociable animal who needs a certain amount of company. A lonely, bored dog shut up by itself all day soon becomes destructive and neurotic.

If these points do not make you reconsider the wish to own a dog, there comes the question of choice. In fact with three hundred or so recognized breeds and the ubiquitous mongrel the choice is practically unlimited. It is better to ask yourself what you need from a dog and what you can afford to give in terms of space, time and money. Every dog treated properly will give you unlimited devotion and loving companionship, but look carefully at the breed that takes your eye and try to see past the charms to the disadvantages. The luxurious coat of some breeds needs daily attention. This can be fun for both you and your dog and grooming obviously gives many people a great deal of satisfaction. However it does take time, so if you are short of time it might be wiser to choose a smooth-coated creature. Flat faced breeds tend to suffer in the heat so if you live in a hot climate it is kinder not to choose such a dog. Flat faced breeds also tend to snore. Whether you find this a minor annoyance of a major irritation depends on your temperament, but it is scarcely something that you can blame the dog for.

Above and right: Dogs like to join in all family activities. They make such good pets because they accept the family as a substitute for pack life. *Below:* Dogs enjoy companionship and comfort. Sportsmen used to think both would be detrimental to a working dog but on the contrary the more a dog is with you the more responsive and willing it is likely to become.

Left: Teaching a dog tricks is
a very good way of strengthening
the bond between the dog
and its owner. In fact this
Pembrokeshire Welsh Corgi
is doing something that comes
quite naturally to any dog,
standing on its hind legs when
something is held out of reach.
Some breeds find this easier
than others and it is by
encouraging the dog to do this
on command, and increasing
the time that it remains standing
upright, that the showman
ends up with his dancing dog.
As this places considerable
strain on the back muscles
it should not be taught until
the dog is adult.

Right, above: To a small child
even a small dog can appear
quite embarrassingly large.
However, familiarity breeds
contempt. Children and dogs
brought up together learn to accept
each other on a friendly basis.
Children unused to animals tend
either to be frightened of them
or to be over effusive which
is frightening for the dog.

Right, below: Ball games enable
a lazy owner to give a dog
a lot of exercise in a very
short while. There is a danger
in overdoing it. Some dogs
become so enthusiastic that they
have a mania for balls and
are forever nagging to have
one thrown. Once this sort
of passion develops it is very
difficult to cure.

Above: The more exercise taken by you and your dog, the better for both of you. Jumping and twisting and chasing are the sort of conditioning given to racing greyhounds to build up muscle and fitness. Although this mongrel will not be going in for the greyhound Derby it is more likely to have a long and healthy life than an over-fed under-exercised animal.

Right: More and more people take the family dog on holiday as a matter of course. Ball games at the seaside always get enthusiastic participation. It is worth giving some thought to the kind of ball you use. Some disintegrate too easily into pieces that are dangerous if they are swallowed by the dog. The size of the ball is also important for it is not unknown for a ball to become lodged in a dog's windpipe causing it to suffocate.

Above: This German Shepherd Dog, preparing to fetch a stick with such enthusiasm would probably be happy to continue all day if given the chance.
Left: It sometimes takes considerable patient training to get a dog to enter the water with speed and confidence. Although all dogs can swim not all of them enjoy it— perhaps because of an alarming experience when they first went into the water. Paddling in the water and encouraging the puppy to follow will help it to gain confidence. As the dog gets bolder swimming will come naturally.

Many dogs learn to swim in their efforts to fetch sticks, and this can happen at any stage. One nine-year-old bitch, who had never entered the water voluntarily, became an enthusiastic swimmer in her efforts to retrieve the ball being thrown for a younger dog of whom she was jealous.

Temperament is something else that is very much a personal choice. Everyone means something different by good temperament. What they really mean by the words is the temperament that suits them. Breeds do tend to have a characteristic temperament as well as a characteristic look. This can only be a generalization as much temperament is man-made and there are always individual dogs to disprove any sweeping statement about a particular breed. Nevertheless most terriers are cheerful, energetic extroverts, often courageous to the point of foolhardiness and inclined to turn a deaf ear to any commands that might interfere with their enjoyment. There are some breeds which contain a large number of individuals which like to be boss. These are dogs of "hard" temperament and they suit owners who like the battle of wills necessary to make this kind of dog obedient. Happy-go-lucky owners may well enjoy the more zany types of dog, while those who like an ordered existence may do better with one of the more biddable breeds.

The family dog has a number of different roles to play in a household. Because the dog is a social animal it will accept the people it is living with as part of the pack. Usually one particular member will be regarded as the pack leader and this will nearly always be whoever spends time teaching the dog. People get many different satisfactions out of owning an animal. Most people enjoy the fuss their dog makes of them. It makes them feel good to receive such uncritical devotion. Many like caring for an animal. To care for something that needs you is a very basic human desire. Critics may sneer that in some situations dogs are patently child substitutes, but it is perhaps better that a dog is cast in this role than that maternal feelings and affections are suppressed completely. Between some couples expressing concern for the dog is the only way they have of showing affection for each other. In other households the dog provides the companionship for the lonely and the mis-understood. There are also situations where the dog is cast in the role of scapegoat on whom the bullied inferior can take out his (or her) own frustrations. In the past man has used the dog as a working animal and the indications are that the dog is just as much needed today though possibly in rather a different role.

Above: Whether in city streets or on the banks of a French canal a dog should be kept under control and on a lead if it is likely to be a danger to itself or a nuisance to others—but where there is a safe opportunity a dog will get much more exercise if it is able to run free.
Below: A pair of Cardigan Welsh Corgis out for their walk.
Left: Dogs must be exercised whatever the weather. A chore which should be shared out around the family.

Many parents like to get a dog for the sake of the children. The whole subject of dogs with children tends to be clouded with sentiment rather than viewed with common sense. Very few children are mature enough to have the unsupervised responsibility of looking after a dog until they are about eleven years old or so. Of course many younger children will derive much pleasure from a dog's company but they should not be expected to cope with the exercise, grooming and feeding on their own, though they should be encouraged to help.

In families without a dog it may be wiser to postpone buying one until the children are of school age. If the bouncy, energetic, six-months-old puppy is of any size it is bound to accidentally knock the toddler flying as well as chewing up all the favorite toys. If the puppy is of a small breed the child is likely to hurt it, again unintentionally, but because the child knows no better.

A child hurt by a dog is excused its fear of animals for the rest of its life, but a dog hurt by a child is not forgiven for showing an equally explicable fear and dislike later on.

A puppy who is introduced into a family with children who have never had a dog before will probably need a certain amount of protection against over handling, but it is by teaching children the fact that young animals need periods of rest and quiet that the seeds of consideration for others are sown. In families where dogs and children are an accepted and unremarkable part of life, the two usually coexist amicably, often in a state of mutual support against the authority of adults. To all who love dogs the ones owned in childhood are unforgettable. Like one's first love affair it is a relationship that can be sought again many times but can never be repeated. It is for this reason that the child deprived of the dog it wants loses an experience that is irreplaceable.

Left: Dogs are creatures of habit so fetching the daily paper or your slippers when you get home can be part of an enjoyable routine for them. Gundogs, like this Irish Setter, have to have "soft mouths"— they should pick things up gently without damaging them. On the whole it is easier to teach this kind of dog to fetch and carry than it is some other breeds.

Below left: Rearing two puppies together is liable to try anyone's patience. The amount of mischief a single puppy can get into is nothing compared with the chaos caused by two! They will also be more difficult to train as one will constantly distract the other. It is probably more sensible for those who want more than one dog to ensure that here is an age gap between them—if they can resist a pair of charmers like these Norwegian Buhunds.

Right: Children need to be quite old before a dog can be left as their sole responsibility. However, there is no more satisfactory relationship than that of a child and dog exploring the countryside together. The dog's sense of smell will discover many things that the boy's eyes would miss.

Acknowledgements

The publisher would like to thank the following for supplying the photographs reproduced in this book:
Australian News and Information Bureau page 66t; Elly Bientema page 9b, 14b, 27, 47b, 67b, 89t, 91t, 91b, 93t; Anne Cumbers page 15b, 16, 17, 21t, 40b, 44b, 53b, 58t, 58b, 64b, 71t, 71b, 75cr, 94b, 95; Robert Estall page 32, 42-43, 44-45; Paul Forrester page 1, 7, 8t, 9t, 15t, 18t, 18b, 19t, 19b, 20tl, 20b, 22tl, 22tr, 22bl, 22br, 24t, 24b, 25t, 25b, 26, 31, 34, 35, 36t, 36c, 36b, 37, 38b, 41t, 41b, 43r, 47t, 55, 56, 59, 62b, 64t, 68b, 70l, 72, 73b, 74tl, 74tr, 74br, 75t, 75br, 75cl, 78t, 79t, 84, 85, 86t, 86b, 87, 88, 90t, 92, 93b; Greyhound Racing Association page 49, 50t, 50b, 51t, 51b, 52-53; 53t; Robert Harding Associates page 10-11; Bill Leimbach page 40t; Howard Loxton page 12b, 90b; John Moss page 14t, 46b, 62t, 63t, 67t, 70r, 77, 78b, 79b, 81t, 82l, 94t; Peter Myers page 38t, 73t; Spectrum Colour Library page 2-3, 6, 12t, 21b, 29t, 45b, 57b, 63b, 82-83, 89b; A. Teasdale page 23; Sally-Anne Thompson page 4-5, 8b, 39, 48, 54, 66b, 68t, 74bl, 75bl; ZEFA page 13, 28, 29b, 30b, 33, 46t, 57t, 61, 64-65, 69b, 80, 81b, 96, jacket; ZEFA/Photri page 69t.

The publisher would also like to thank the following dog owners for making their dogs available for photography:
Mr Attwood for the St Bernard on page 73; Mr Brampton for the Chihuahua and the Chinese Crested on page 75; Mrs Dean for the Keeshond on page 84; Mrs M. Fielden for the Pyrenean Mountain Dog on page 36; Mr P. Grout and Mr I. Kellam for the Corgi on pages 86 and 88; Mrs Hargrave for the Borzois on pages 38 and 74; Mrs G. Heath for the Dalmatian on page 34; Mrs Sarah Jane for the Afghan Hounds on pages 41 and 55; Mr Morgan for the Mastiff on page 72; Mrs Powell-Wheatley for the Gordon Setters on pages 59 and 85; Mr Sameja for the Yorkshire Terrier on page 19; Mrs Thomas for the Bulldog on page 56; Miss V. Warman for the Maltese on page 18; Mrs Young for the Pekingese on page 75.

The Publishers have attempted to observe the legal requirements with respect to the rights of the suppliers of photographic materials. Nevertheless, persons who have claims are invited to apply to the Publishers.